Dimensions of Moral Creativity

Dimensions of Moral Creativity

Paradigms, Principles, and Ideals

A. S. Cua

The Pennsylvania State University Press

University Park and London

Acknowledgments

I am grateful to the editors and publishers of the following journals for permission to use previously published materials: *The American Philosophical Quarterly, Ethics, Inquiry, Man and World, The New Scholasticism, Philosophy East and West,* and *Proceedings of the American Catholic Philosophical Association.*

Library of Congress Cataloging in Publication Data

Cua, Antonio S
   Dimensions of moral creativity.

   Includes bibliography and index.
   1. Ethics. I. Title.
BJ1012.C8   170   77-16169
ISBN 0-271-00540-8

In memory of my father-in-law
Khaw Boon-Teng
(1894–1973)
whose life embodied *jên, li,* and *i*

Preface

This inquiry deals with the nature of moral experience from the view-point of a reflective agent. It explores, in particular, the creative aspect of the moral life by focusing on the role of paradigmatic individuals as concrete embodiments of principles and ideals. For exemplifying this role an excursion is made to Confucian ethics. Throughout this exploration, I am concerned with moral understanding rather than justification of claims to moral knowledge. I thus employ relatively fluid notions to emphasize the different dimensions of moral creativity without pretending to offer a systematic theory.

The present work bears the marks of learning, encouragement, and inspiration from my teachers Professor Karl Aschenbrenner and the late Professor Stephen C. Pepper. My colleagues and friends Paul Weiss, Kenneth Schmitz, and Nicholas Rescher have contributed much in responding to the germinal ideas present in this work. Any errors and inadequacies, however, are entirely my own. I owe a special debt to Dean Jude P. Dougherty, School of Philosophy, the Catholic University of America, for his personal interest, encouragement, and support, and the provision of secretarial assistance in the preparation of this work for publication. Thanks are also due to Professor William V. Grimes, the State University of New York at Albany, and Professor Ralph M. McInerny, the University of Notre Dame, for their valuable suggestions in the revision of the manuscript, and to Carole Schwager for her editorial assistance.

My Chinese studies have been helped greatly by the encouragement of Wing-tsit Chan, Chung-ying Cheng, and Siu-chi Huang. To my wife Shoke-hwee Khaw, I am deeply grateful for her untiring concern and critical comments on all my Confucian works. Finally, I am appreciative of my daughter Athene for her understanding and affection during all the years of my preoccupation with the present project.

Contents

Introduction

A. The Problem of Moral Creativity

We begin our exploration of the nature of moral agency by focusing upon the interplay of two aspects of the situation in which moral problems arise. The situation may be characterized as a personal predicament that calls for a decision as to what to do in respect to the problem at issue. It is also a situation in which a reasonable agent deploys certain principles or rules as reasons in support of his decision. This aspect has received central emphasis in recent Anglo-American moral philosophy. The task for philosophy is seen primarily as examination of the logic of moral discourse and study of the logical behavior of moral concepts involved in practical reasoning. The significance of a moral practice as an interpersonal setting of rules and principles lies in its presumptive warrant for nonarbitrary decisions and actions. This setting is of both moral and philosophical interest, since principles and rules license the reason-giving process. The interest in moral reasoning justly calls attention to the importance of the need to have a conceptual understanding of moral discourse prior to any attempt at constructing moral norms that may aid ordinary agents in the resolution of practical moral problems and perplexities.

The interplay of the two aspects of moral situation is stressed in Hare's notion of a "decision of principles."[1] Moral principles, being action guides, are universalizable. The emerging picture of the moral situation informs us of one aspect of the agent's decision-making process in light of the principles which he accepts as guides to conduct. The notion of decisions of principles suggests the central theme of this book, for implicit in the notion is a focus on the possibility of origination of new principles for action. Hare says that "all decisions except those, if any, that are completely arbitrary are to some extent decisions of principles. We are always setting precedents for ourselves . . . decisions and principles interact throughout the whole field."[2] This remark suggests our problem of moral creativity or pioneering, although the suggestion is restrictive in terms of the exclusive framework of moral principles. Creative agency is viewed solely in terms of the manner in which a moral agent qualifies the function of moral principles in coping with his situations. An interesting question remains: Given an established moral practice as embodying a set of rules that governs behavior, how is the moral practice modified by the agent's decisions of principles? What sorts of consideration enter into this process of moral change? Are there personal valuational factors that affect the nature and function of the moral practice that one should attend to in an attempt to understand the nature of creative moral agency? The legalistic or rule model of creative agency, in stressing decisions of principles as precedents, tends to be too formal. As Mayo points out, "The ethics of moral principles, with its emphasis on universality, assimilates the moral agent to the citizen."[3] This restrictive model of creative agency is a natural consequence in the ethics of moral principles. It unduly limits the notion of morality to the realm of norms that govern interpersonal relationship. Other dimensions of creative agency tend to be ignored. There are, for instance, the dimension of "saints and heroes" and the plurality of personal moral standards that guide an agent's conduct, which may affect the character and function of moral principles.[4] Strawson has drawn our attention to the "region of the ethical" as a region of conflicting ideals and images of man that seize upon moral agents for competing allegiance.[5] It appears arbitrary to rule them out as insignificant intrusions upon moral practice. These various emphases on other facets of moral creativity speak to the need for a broader conception of morality in which moral rules and principles form only a part of the central core.

A broader conception of creative moral agency does not deny the legitimacy and insights of the analytic task. The rule model of morality, though restrictive in conception, does contribute to our understanding of the practical character of moral reasoning and the nature of moral concepts. Moreover, some recent philosophers, inspired by Continental existentialism, have insisted on the need to replace the rule model of moral creativity in order to focus upon the aspect of decision as involving the inner life of the moral agent: "the texture of a man's being or the nature of his personal vision."[6] The radical suggestion is that we replace the rule model by the model of the painter to properly appreciate moral creativity.[7] The plea is to see morality, from beginning to end, as a personal affair. According to this view, morality is more of an art than a science. "In art and morality alike both tradition and innovation can find honourable places. . . . The one need not be a dead hand any more than the other need lead to anarchy. The originality which is important is not necessarily novelty but a kind of unpredictable freshness for which no recipe can be given."[8] In this perspective, to understand moral agents we need to focus upon the creative manner in which a person's moral outlook is exemplified in conduct. Creative moral agency cannot be captured by a single analytical model of principles and rules.

For a reflective moral agent attempting to understand the nature of his moral life, both the rule model and the artist model provide perspectives to view the aspects of moral agency. The two models, construed as exclusive pictures of creative agency, tend to be restrictive. The rule model, if used in an exclusive way, tends to have a narrow view of the interpersonal setting of the moral situation, for significant creative forms of decision appear to be intelligible only against the background of a moral practice. If moral decisions are not to be arbitrary inventions of principles, they must have some sort of continuity or relation to a preexisting moral practice. We need a preliminary map of moral experience in which the different models complement one another, a map not only for the logic of moral reasoning, but also for the logic of application of moral principles in light of personal factors that interact with moral decisions. The central theme of this book revolves around the problem of moral creativity, i.e., the possible contributions of a moral agent to his moral practice. In this inquiry we adopt a broader conception of morality and moral creativity, embracing both the insight of the rule model of morality in its stress on the dimension of principles and rules and the insight of the artist model in its stress on the dimension of personal ideals and standards that enter into the valuative experience of the agent in the process of commitment and performance. In this exploration we are concerned not directly with principled moral judgments, conventionally understood, but with the range of personal valuative acts: modes of being that constitute and create, so to speak, personhood.

In considering three dimensions of moral creativity we deal with a variety of related topics with the aim of providing a preliminary sketch rather than blueprints of moral creativity. The problem of moral creativity is seen primarily as a problem of the dynamics of the moral life. The various dimensions discussed do not have equal weight for all moral agents. In this exploration, I adopt the position of a reflective agent who seeks to understand the nature of his agency in relation to a moral practice which he accepts and lives his life. In an inquiry of this sort, it is inevitable that certain personal sentiments enter the process of reflection. In this regard, our exploration of the central theme is, to some extent, tied up with an exegesis of the author's fundamental beliefs about the nature of morality. In Chapter 1 I attempt to articulate and clarify the nature of this approach in relation to two different types of ethical inquiries.

B. Two Points of View of Moral Reflection and Moral Creativity

The position of a reflective agent that underlies our inquiry is the internal rather than the external point of view of a moral practice.[9] The rules that are embedded in a moral practice are thus seen to be endowed with an authoritative force recognized by the reflective agent. From the position of a reflective agent, the moral rules or principles may be viewed in two ways, the *retrospective* and *prospective* points of view. Retrospectively, the agent is interested primarily in judging or assessing his actual or contemplated performance. The interpersonal setting of moral rules is deemed a framework for the regulation and evaluation of conduct. We call this point of view "retrospective," not in the literal sense of that term, but in the sense that actions, whether actual or contemplated, are regarded as acts possessing determinate properties resembling the character of past deeds, situations, and events. Philosophers have focused on the central problem of moral justification. This presupposes that morality is a rational affair: that reasons the agents give in support of their judgments and conduct exhibit a conceptual structure of moral rules and concepts. Moral rules and concepts thus function as categories for classifying moral performance into various types.

Recent moral philosophy has much to contribute to our understanding of the nature of a moral agent in the role of a moral judge of conduct. To distinguish this retrospective from a prospective point of view, consider an actual situation of moral problem or perplexity. Prospectively, the agent is concerned with what he will do, not merely in terms of his governing moral principles, but in light of the question "What will I be?" The substance of his moral practice, in this perspective, does not always offer clear and definitive guidance. The artist model of moral agency justly stresses the importance of this question of being. And it is illuminating to see that an agent's answer to this question may still be meaningful even if it does not appeal to moral principles. The artist model draws our attention to the complexity of moral agency that seem to resist understanding in terms of a single model.

The two points of view of a reflective agent initially aid us in understanding moral creativity. From the retrospective point of view, much of our creativity would be confined to the modification of moral rules through the enlarging or narrowing of their scope of operation. In this regard, we need to distinguish the *form* from the *content* of morality. The logic of moral reasoning restricts its task to the form by stressing the universalizing and action-guiding character of moral reasoning. The content of morality in this way remains quite fluid. However, if moral rules are regarded as open textured with no rigid preestablished boundaries of application, the moral agent may have to interpret the significance of these moral rules in his deliberation within the setting of his problematic situations. The content of the moral practice may seem to an agent to embrace various sorts of items lurking in the background of his moral learning. These items, conveniently termed "moral rules," may consist of general principles, precepts, specific injunctions addressed to concrete situations, or abstract examples of application of moral rules. In a morally problematic situation, a reflective agent may have to make up his mind as to what constitutes a relevant consideration. In coming to cope with his personal problem, he may, in effect, be reconstituting the content of his moral practice in a manner not anticipated by the normal functioning of moral rules. His decisions in these problematic circumstances do not necessarily entail an acceptance by his fellow agents. In any case, his decisions do have a projective possibility of acceptance by others insofar as they are seen to be congruent with the intent of his moral practice. His decisions may become paradigms for other agents who confront similar predicaments. When this in fact occurs, the agent may be a moral pioneer, thus contributing in a modest way to his moral practice.

From the prospective point of view not tied to the content of the moral practice, the moral agent can also contribute to the life of a moral practice insofar as his decision and performance are seen in relation to his ideals and styles of life. The manner in which he brings his ideals to bear on the moral practice may become a paradigm for other agents. Morality, in this regard, is the home of diversity of creative contributions. And in an open society, it is a dynamic process in which various reconstitutive and ideally based performances compete for dialectical resolution and acceptance. The complexity of moral life may ultimately lie in this region of creative competition of ideal commitments within a communal framework of a moral practice in which individual decisions may be seen as part of its implication.

In this book I gather a series of explorations that focus on moral creativity from both the retrospective and the prospective points of view of moral agency. It presents *a* record of one moral agent's reflections on the nature of morality. After a preliminary exposition of the approach that underlies our journey, in Chapter 2 we take up a central question on the nature of moral actuation or of the transformative significance of an established moral practice. This question, I believe, can in part receive some light through an inquiry into the role and significance of the paradigmatic individuals or exemplary agents in various moral practices. Chapters 3, 4, and 5 are devoted to this task. In Chapter 4 we make an excursion to the ethics of Confucius in order to provide an example of an ethics that explicitly recognizes the role of paradigmatic individuals. Chapter 6 turns to the question of the relation between moral rules and particular circumstances that confront moral agents. One type of agent's decision involves an appeal to ideals and styles of life—a topic which we pursue in Chapter 7.

In Chapter 8 we conclude our journey by a discussion of the distinction between two interpretations of moral ideals and their relevance to the question of the meaning of one's life. In this terminal part of our journey, I suggest that the question of the search for the meaning of one's life is a prospective question that relates to ideals and styles of life. Moral creativity is finally understood in terms of the capacity of the moral agent to answer his original question of actuation. I do not aim to present a theory of moral creativity, but rather to present the landscape as embedded with three dimensions of experience that may interweave in the life of particular moral agents.

This book is in part an experiment in self-understanding and in part a philosophical attempt at understanding the process of envisagement of ideals and responding with commitment that lies at the heart of the enterprise of creative moral agency. I hope it will also aid concerned moral agents in their effort at a practical understanding of the nature of their moral experience.

1

Moral Creativity as a
Task of Self-Understanding

A. Cartography of Morals

A reflective agent, in attempting to understand the nature of his moral experience, may receive light from two different types of moral inquiry: the epistemology and the cartography of morals. The epistemology of morals aims at an adequate account of moral justification. It is primarily addressed to the interpersonal setting of moral judgments. Since moral judgments of reflective agents make claim to objectivity and validity, they presuppose a social or public framework of assessment. One task of moral inquiry, whether normative or analytical, is concerned with the justificatory credentials that underlie ethical claims. The task in part is devoted to the classification of different kinds of ethical claims and the provision of criteria for the assessment of these claims. In stressing the interpersonal setting, an epistemology of morals is likely to neglect factors that are often of paramount importance to the lives of individual agents. The enterprise, centering on the nature of moral appraisal and justification, can be supplemented by a cartography of morals, which would reflect the aim of understanding morality apart from a concern with the problem of justification. It would not replace the intrinsic importance of the epistemic investigation of moral beliefs and moral concepts used in the acts and processes of appraisal.

Our aim in understanding moral creativity is related to the cartography rather than the epistemology of morals. Initially we need to make clear the nature of this sort of moral inquiry. As the term suggests, a cartography of morals has to do with the mapping of the various features of the territory of moral experiences. Applying the technique of mapmaking to moral experience, we may distinguish two different types of cartography of morals (henceforth CM). In one we can construe a CM as an attempt to make a comprehensive survey of the terrain of the moral life by mapping out its basic and subordinate features in one synoptic view. This sort of CM belongs to a general theory of value. If this activity is to be successful, all the detailed features of the moral life must be charted without ambiguity. In a way, such a CM does not help a reflective agent in understanding his own life, since the features mapped may appear to be static items with relatively enduring relationships. It seems that the problem of reflective understanding is more concerned with the changing relationship between the charted items of moral experience in the lives of individual agents. It is a theoretic ideal for a CM to offer a complete understanding of the moral life by mapping out all the items and their actual and possible relationships. But this ideal, if carried out, is likely to acquire a static and abstract character that may fail to do justice to the dynamics of individual moral experiences. Whether such an inquiry is illuminating to a particular reflective agent depends on how he experiences the world rather than on a theoretical prescription of the nature of moral experiences in general.

As distinct from a *comprehensive* CM, an inquirer may engage in a more modest *selective* CM. Calling a CM an art of mapmaking suggests in one basic sense "art" defined as "human effort to imitate, supplement, alter, or counteract the works of nature." Let us use this notion as a guide in explaining the nature of a selective CM.

1. As an effort or activity of imitation, a selective CM must be faithful to the original objects of imitation. In this sense, the moral experiences of different agents form the raw material that must in some way be depicted in the map of moral experiences. But this depicting process should not be viewed in terms of isomorphism or one-to-one correspondence of the depicting features and their original items. Since it is doubtful whether there is a comprehensive sense of "moral experience" that is applicable to all human beings, a selective CM should be concerned with depicting the *dominant* features within the domain of moral experiences. The term "dominant" is a term of judgment. It signifies the inquirer's *decision of selectivity,* i.e., a decision or judgment to focus on the "noteworthy" or "remarkable" features of moral experiences that seem to pervade the different cultural settings of the moral life. What is imitated or depicted on the map is in effect a judgment of what is worthy of depiction on the map. In this sense, a selective CM cannot be normatively innocent, for it betrays certain normative commitments, at least, as preparatory commitments at the originating stage of inquiry.

These preparatory commitments, moreover, do not constitute the criteria for assessing the adequacy of a selective CM, but they do point to the lack of normative and methodological neutrality. However, this lack of normative innocence need not preclude a CM from being illuminating to reflective moral agents, just as an art of imitation does not preclude it from having aesthetic value.

2. Let us turn to the second activity or effort of supplementation. To the extent to which our depicting activity in 1 is colored by a decision of selectivity, one brings into his CM inquiry certain supplementary features, i.e., by completing what is deemed incomplete, explicating what is merely implicit in ordinary moral experiences. The noted features of our ordinary experiences, for instance, may be incomplete in the sense that the selected features have no implicit boundaries. We may attempt, then, to delineate these boundaries, thus in a sense completing the incomplete terrain of the moral life.

3. Regarding the third sort of effort or activity of alteration, to what extent the supplementary activity of a selective CM is deemed an alteration is an open question. There is little doubt that a successful supplementation may yield the consequence in altering the terrain of moral experiences, not so much in the sense that the mapped items are altered, but in the sense that the items, owing to the supplementary activity, may be viewed in a new light. The moral geography is thereby altered in significance in light of emphasis and elucidation.

4. A selective CM, in focusing upon dominant features of the moral life, may also bring about certain notions in describing the various features that may appear to be unfamiliar to ordinary moral experiences. If an agent adopts these notions, his uses of these notions may involve giving up certain linguistic habits and associated assumptions. A work of elucidating moral experience may end up in counteracting certain assumptions and beliefs which a reflective agent deems natural to hold. However, no selective CM can eliminate the vital features embedded in ordinary thinking, for its aim is to understand, and not to judge, what ought to enter into an agent's orbit of moral experiences. In this sense, a selective CM does not prescribe the features of moral experience. It can bring certain features to light by emphasis or deemphasis, but it cannot eliminate them.

A selective cartography of morals is no doubt an art. Its usefulness depends on the illuminating focus or the central and pervasive features of moral experiences rather than on a detailed taxonomy of the moral life. As distinct from an epistemology of morals, a selective cartography of morals need not pretend to any discovery of universal truths. It can contend with, to borrow a phrase from the later Wittgenstein, "assemblages of reminders for particular purposes." In this book, our concern with understanding the nature of moral creativity is related to a selective cartography of morals. Although I do not propose to offer such a cartography, what we focus on in our exploration may yield features that will enter into a more general enterprise of understanding the nature of the moral life.[1]

B. Three Focal Notions

In this inquiry I occasionally employ certain terms as conceptual tools for understanding moral creativity. These terms are intended primarily as focal devices or lenses for stressing different dimensions of moral creativity. Since these terms are not to be construed as descriptive, classificatory, or explanatory concepts, it is best to call them *focal notions*. Such focal notions do not pretend to set forth the conceptual structure of moral experience, although a detailed systematic explication of their uses may furnish data for an adequate philosophy of the moral life. However, whether or not they yield this conceptual fruit remains an open question that lies beyond the scope of this book. We are at present uncertain about the theoretical promise of these notions. Perhaps a closer study of these focal notions in relation to moral concepts may throw light upon the nature of the moral life as a whole. For the time being we are concerned only with their role in a selective CM, for it is most difficult to conduct such an enterprise without the use of at least some analogous focal notions in mapping out the crucial features of moral experiences.

This section presents a preliminary discussion of three focal notions employed in this work. These notions are often used in an intuitive way, which may cause the reader some confusion, but I believe they will be clarified progressively in proper contexts that call for a more elaborate rather than an intuitive understanding of their uses. We thus avoid definitions, since definitions are liable to suggest that we have categorial concepts to classify the different dimensions of moral creativity. This is not to imply that our focal notions are free from conceptual criticism. It is quite possible that we should employ other focal notions, since many of our terms are found in the current vocabulary with no consistent uses. However, I have chosen to revise the familiar notions rather than offer technical terminologies, for familar notions do seem to focus, though not obeying the law of consistent linguistic use, upon features of moral experience that require attention from moral philosophers.

The three notions to be discussed are form of life, way of life, and style of life. All these notions will be further elaborated in relation to relevant topics.[2] The term "life" underlies the connection of these three notions. This should not be surprising since our focal notions have to do with the valuative life of individual moral agents. The notion of life reminds us of the underlying theme of moral creativity.

Form of life.   The notion of a form of life owes its use to Wittgenstein, who remarked that "what has to be accepted, the given, is—so one could say 'forms of life.' "[3] To understand the moral life, we need to be aware of what is the given—the "framework" in which the participants share certain moral attitudes, feelings, and judgments. Agreement in a form of life underlies the intelligibility of moral discourse. Wittgenstein's insight, in spite of the lack of perspicuity in the sort of framework he has in mind, may be applied to ethics. I suggest that we use the notion of a form of life as a focal lens on the *background* of moral acceptance. It is the background of our moral practice that makes intelligible the uses of moral concepts. We may regard this background as a reservoir of shared moral intentions which commitive agents may draw on for moral judgments and decisions, particularly in cases where the moral rules do not offer explicit guidance. Focus upon the background of the moral life does not mean that if moral agents are reminded of certain moral problems or perplexities they will offer uniform moral judgments or responses to them. Conscious attention to a system of shared attitudes may bring with it a certain judgment or decision on the character of the background. This is one of the insights in Mayo's work: morality involves both a consensual and a dissensual aspect. The consensual aspect is a presupposition of a shared form of life that renders moral speech intelligible. But this reminder does not guarantee actual consensus in judgment and performance. Actual dissensus is thus compatible with this consensual background. There is one possible explanation here: the moral concepts we use in discourse and deliberation are open rather than complete notions.[4] Although their use presupposes a framework of intelligibility, they do not completely describe or classify moral acts and attitudes with a degree of precision and determinateness that one would expect from concepts in general. Moral concepts sometimes function more like labels or cap-fitting devices (to borrow a term from Austin)

rather than classificatory categories.[5] Moral agents do confront problems and perplexities in the various situations in their lives. The uncertain or exigent situations are not labeled so that the moral agents can
readily identify and classify them. Hampshire reminds us that "the situations in which we must act or abstain from acting are 'open' in the sense
that they cannot be uniquely described and finally circumscribed. Situations do not present themselves with their labels attached to them; if they
did, practical problems would be conclusively soluble theoretical problems . . . the crux is in the labelling, or the decision depends on how we
see the situations."[6]

How the moral agent labels his situation constitutes his view of the
situation, and for *him* constitutes the nature of his situation. If he appeals
to the background to sustain his view, his belief concerning the nature of
the background may form part of his conception of his form of life,
which he admittedly shares with fellow agents. The form of life as a
background of a moral life that renders intelligible moral speech and
performance is thus an *existential matrix* in which moral agents live. The
cognitive expression of the form of life depends on the view of individual agents concerning the nature of the matrix in which his life revolves.
In using the notion of a form of life, we simply draw attention to this
shared existential matrix of morality without proposing a cognitive account for its constitutive nature. Perhaps a metaphor may be helpful in
clarifying our focal notion. This is the metaphor of "atmosphere." Each
moral practice seems to be pervaded with an atmosphere. A person who
lives in a form of life, in confronting an alien practice, can sense and feel
the atmosphere in which an alien moral practice operates. It is a sort of
feeling that a group of moral agents who adhere to a moral practice
belongs to a community, possessing, as it were, a sense of common anchorage upon an inchoate background. Experiences of "culture shocks"
for moral agents who encounter an alien morality perhaps give us an
understanding of the difference between two forms of life or modes of
moral existence.[7] Forms of life, to use a distinction of Russell's, are more
objects of acquaintance than of description.[8] We are familiar with a form
of life through an experiential encounter rather than through a set of
descriptive propositions. It is an "atmosphere" in which moral agents
live, not a conceptual framework of their moral existence.[9]

Ways of life.   The notion of a way of life enables an observer of moral
community to talk in some coherent way about an agent's or a group of
agents' system of moral beliefs and performances. Whenever a group of

agents who live within a community judge and behave in some convergent fashion and explain their judgments and behavior as compliant with a set of rules, we may refer to them as having a way of life or a *moral practice*.[10] This use of the notion of a way of life is analogous to the anthropologists' use of "cultural pattern" or "cultural way of life." Since I do not intend to propose an account of cultural patterns in this work, I prefer the use of the notion of a moral practice as synonymous with the notion of a communal way of life. The morality of a community, describable in terms of a set of rules and regulations, "consists of those ways of behavior which each member of the community is taught, bidden and encouraged to adopt by other members." In this sense, moral behavior is "behavior in accordance with these recommended patterns, moral grounds are grounds derived from applying accepted rules, moral issues are issues involving the required standards."[11]

The notion of a moral practice or communal way of life is used to focus upon the coherent and convergent ways of behaving as congruent with a set of *formulable* rules. The coherence or convergence we discern in a moral community, however, need not correspond to the lived patterns of individual moral agents, for many moral practices are open rather than closed systems of rules with a preestablished ordering of precedence and importance. More often moral agents, particularly the reflective ones, are likely to bring into their own judgment and performance features of moral import not previously given by moral practice. Thus within a communal way of life, there may be a diversity of *individual* ways of life—diverse patterns or individual modes of existence with a common tie to a preestablished practice. For one thing, a moral agent, though committed to the authoritative force of a set of moral rules, may still need to exercise rulings or make decisions on the relevance of rules to *his* concrete circumstance. The situation, particularly the exigent one, may not be one that comfortably fits in with the normal function of these rules. As previously noted, how the moral agent labels the situation depends on his view of the situation. A moral practice is in this way *open* to individual construction in the sense that the content of the practice is subject to reconstitution by moral agents in particular cases. This emphasis on the reconstitutive process of moral agency within a moral practice gives us an understanding of one dimension of moral creativity, for it brings with it an attention to the *ways* in which an individual interiorizes and integrates the given content of a morality within his mode of existence. The variability of individual ways of life may thus be understood in terms of the factors that influence an agent's process of reconstituting the content of his moral practice. If these observations are correct, the coherence we discern and ascribe to a moral practice need not entail corresponding coherence on the part of the individual agents who live within the moral practice.

In brief, the notion of a way of life may be used in both the communal and the individual sense. In the communal sense, we equate a way of life with a moral practice as the interpersonal or common setting of moral rules that govern the behavior of a community. In a sense, a moral practice admits of a diversity of ways of life in the individual sense. Moral creativity may in part be understood in terms of these individual ways of life with a tie to a moral practice. It has been suggested that a "way of life" be defined as a "set of value systems each of which belongs to a different point of view and all of which are arranged in an order of relative precedence."[12] I have not followed this suggestion since, in my view, a moral practice, though a system of a sort, is a relatively "loose" system in which the question of precedence of rules is open to individual interpretation and decision. What import a moral rule has depends on how the agent construes its function as relevant to his situation rather than decisively established by the mere acknowledgment of the force of the moral rule. However, Taylor's notion is a useful one in focusing on the ways of life of highly rational beings.

More needs to be said about individual ways of life. Leaving aside the question of relative precedence in moral practice, we can still regard some individual ways of life as being dominated by a certain ideal telos or policy of life. This is one of the central insights of Aristotle's *Nicomachean Ethics*. To understand an individual way of life we may profitably focus upon the dominant aim (or aims) that appear to direct the agent's life. His telos is an ordering principle of a sort. Thus how an individual orders and integrates his emotions, desires, needs, and aspirations may furnish us a clue to his way of life. However, our ascription of a dominating telos is subject to defeat by an act of individual disavowal, for a man's life may be dominated by a plurality of ends without the coherence that an observer ascribes to him. Thus our characterization of his way of life may not coincide with how he views it. But to draw attention to this possible discrepancy between ascription and personal avowal need not detract from the usefulness of the notion of a way of life in focusing upon the variable sorts of considerations and factors that enter into a characterization of an individual's moral life, though an ascriber of ends, particularly the ideal ones, need be aware of the defeasible nature of his ascriptions.

Styles of life.   This is again a familiar notion often used interchangeably with the other two notions discussed. This term is used here as a distinct focal notion stressing the qualitative aspects of an agent's life and performance. Like individual ways of life, we may speak of a style of life as being dominated by a certain telos. The heart of the distinction lies in a contrast between two interpretations of moral ideals elucidated in Chapter 8. The notion of style of life is meant to suggest a distinction between the descriptive *content* and *quality* of individual modes of existence. When we choose to speak of the content of a life in the way in which it is organized into a pattern of beliefs and performances, we focus on the ways of life; when we choose to focus on the qualitative significance of a way of life, we propose to use the notion of a style of life. An aesthetic analogy may be useful in explaining our notions. A work of art, say a painting, can be characterized in terms of the ways in which various elements are ordered in an overall artistic design, or it can be regarded as an expression of an excellent qualitative *gestalt.* In the latter perspective, we may speak of the quality or excellence of a work of art. The notion of quality or style of a work, in the idiosyncratic sense, is what enables us to identify and distinguish it from other works. The notion of style here is not used in the art historian's sense, for we use it as a focal rather than a classificatory notion. Nor is the notion of quality used in the sense of attribute or property. Attributes and properties can be applied to more than two distinct individuals, but the notion of quality merely focuses upon the idiosyncratic character of the individual. We may see individual works of art as being dominated by different styles or qualities in the idiosyncratic sense yet sharing in the same generic content characterizable in terms of common properties or attributes. Analogously, we may see individual modes of existence as exemplifying different styles of life, although their content or ways of life may appear to have the same characterization. The ends of the ways of life need not be exclusive properties of distinctive persons. With styles of life, however, we focus upon the idiosyncratic features of identity of the personal mode of existence. It is this idiosyncratic identity that appears to give meaning or significance to a person's life. Thus we may also speak of the qualitative significance of a way of life, i.e., the style of life.

Like the notion of a way of life, style of life admits of both an

individual and a communal application. Thus one may also use the
notion of a cultural style of life. This is a specially prominent feature of
Confucian morality that is discussed in Chapters 4 and 5. Confucian
morality, as Hsün-tzu rightly saw, is predominantly a ritual morality in
the communal sense.[13] The role of *li* or propriety is a stress on the
importance of a cultural style of life which Confucian agents are urged
to realize. Some anthropologists have found use for this notion. There
is no doubt that styles of life are often idiosyncratic achievements of
men, particularly those we term "paradigmatic individuals"; thus we
can also speak of a cultural style of life or a style of civilization. To the
question "How far is it justified, and how far profitable, to extend the
concept of style to total cultures?" Kroeber offers the following answer:
"This might mean, first and most conservatively, an assembly of all the
several styles occurring in a civilization, with due consideration of their
interactions and inter-influencings. Second, it is conceivable that these
interactions produce something like a superstyle in its own right, and
that this is definable or at least describable."[14] In our inquiry, excepting
for the excursion to Confucian ethics, we do not use the notion of
communal style of life as a focal notion, since it does not seem to have a
significant role to play in our understanding of moral creativity. It is,
however, possible that if it is intelligible to speak of a cultural life style,
there may also be a great idiosyncratic diversity of individual styles of
life within a cultural style of life. This at any rate seems to be the case
with Confucian China.

   To sum up, the various guiding notions we employ in this exploration
are intended primarily as focal lenses to view the various features of
moral creativity. The use of these focal notions does not entail either
specific moral views or conceptual systemic consequences, although their
use reflects certain decisions of selectivity. These focal notions may be
taken as conceptual recommendations for the study of moral creativity,
and I believe they are important to a selective cartography of morals.

C. Understanding Moral Creativity

The three focal notions, in addition to others to be introduced, are
guiding tools to understanding moral creativity. Some remarks on the
notion of understanding as distinct from the notion of explanation will
be helpful here. Unlike discussions of the epistemology of morals, we

generally avoid issues relating to moral justification and reasoning. This is a deliberate strategy on my part since this book is concerned more with what might be called a cognitive appreciation of moral creativity, more with "what it is" than "how it is to be explained and justified." As von Wright recently pointed out, there is a sense of understanding that is distinct from explanation or the "why" question.[15] Adopting this distinction, we may say that our concern with moral creativity relates to the question "What is moral creativity?" and not "Why are there facts of moral creativity?" Inevitably this concern of understanding does involve interpretations. Following von Wright's suggestion, we may call this concern an *explication*. In this sense, our inquiry into the various dimensions of moral creativity is an example of explication. There is little doubt that this activity is a problematic enterprise, for much vagueness infects the phenomenon of moral creativity. What we here hope to achieve is to use focal notions in drawing attention to the interesting features of moral creativity that are often ignored by moral theory. Perhaps the vagueness of the phenomenon is of a systematic sort so that we can finally focus on very few features without a conceptual distortion of the phenomenon. Perhaps an adequate explication needs the use of complementary models of explication, and the result may simply be a convergence of emphasis in the uses of these models. Our use of focal notions perhaps will suggest these models. These focal notions, as previously noted, may serve as a basis for a more complete explication but do not entail any specific sets of descriptions. Our purpose is to shift the direction of understanding in terms of explanation to the activity of explication. The success of this enterprise need not carry any "theoretic weight" in any systematic sense, although the uses of focal notions may have some "theoretic promise." The focal notions can claim no theoretical significance beyond their possible theoretical promises. The features we uncover in our journey may finally figure as important ingredients in a selective cartography of morals. This also is a hope rather than a promise.

Since we are pursuing these studies from the reflective position of a moral agent, what we take to be the nature of moral creativity may be biased by my own moral interests and background. This personal prepossession is here explicitly acknowledged. But I believe that a philosophical exploration of this sort can be useful both to moral philosophy and to the agent who seeks an understanding of his moral life. This notion of philosophical activity we assume to be of legitimate interest to the exercise of our mental life, without claiming it to be an exclusive function of philosophy. This notion points to a basic intellectual motivation that may be regarded as an experiment of some sort. We may call it an "experiment in paradigmity," which has a close affinity with the notion of an "experiment in generalization" familiar in creative intellectual life and discourse.

In engaging in the exercise of our mental capacity and disposition, we are at least initially beset by problems that instigate our intellectual activity. The rehearsal of alternative solutions to problems is intentionally directed to solutions which possess an implicit claim to universality. In both science and philosophy, men are engaged in the experiment in generalization, in exploring the possibility of universal theses to which the title "truth" may be properly awarded. A contrasting activity of experiments in paradigmity, however, lays no claim to a discovery of universal truths, but merely suggests the projection of the terminus of one's experiment as a paradigm for future explorations. A reflective activity conducted with this intention does not therefore aim at the proposal of theses or truth claims. If moral theory can in part be conducted as a process of self-understanding, it is intrinsically personal in its quest. What saves it from being a mere idiosyncratic quest lies in its experiment in paradigmity. One's self-understanding can in this way be a paradigm for another person's self-understanding. The author, as it were, is a speaker, who, if he is successful in his speech, can function also as a *representative speaker*. The audience he addresses must respond to the speaker's speech acts in understanding. But the author's exploration itself need not ask for acceptance by others. His speech has its own integrity, standing for a linguistic expression of his character of reflection. Moreover, from the standpoint of the audience, who rightly assume that the author has something worthwhile to say, even in the saying of it the author clothes it in his personal style, so that the possibility of the speech being a successful experiment in paradigmity seems to be inherent in this sort of discourse. But the author himself, though he thereby offers his signature, cannot certify his own speech as a paradigm without acceptance by the audience. For in truth, the author possesses no credentials to attest to his own authority, unless one regards being a human being as a criterion for significant speech.

Moreover, from the conceptual standpoint, the experiment in paradigmity cannot remain solely a personal one, for speech involves the use of concepts, which are ineluctably a topic for cognitive assessment in discourse. The experiment calls for justification from the point of view of a judge who possesses appropriate canons for judgment. To meet this sort of demand, an experiment in paradigmity may in part be regarded as a *conceptual experiment,* for the exploration on this view is an exploration in conceptual understanding. And for conceptual understanding to gain a rational footing, it must be able to dress itself in general terms that resemble thesis-propounding philosophy. However, it must be noted that conceptual understanding needs a concrete home for the manifestation of its illuminating power. The concrete home of morality is, as we shall see, the home of the paradigmatic individuals—the exemplary moral agents who may be said to have successfully conducted the experiment in paradigmity. In this way, the two notions of experiment distinguished earlier can be seen to have an intimate connection, without depriving the integrity of each in an actual piece of self-understanding by a reflective moral agent. When an experiment in paradigmity is deemed successful and has gained acceptance, as a consequence of such an acceptance, its conclusions can function as general declarations: it can be regarded as a successful experiment in generalization. The two sorts of experiment need not be exclusively hostile to each other. Experiment in generalization may also set up paradigms for future inquiries without proclaiming timeless truths. In the last analysis, insight into one's moral life depends on the acknowledgment of the link between these two sorts of mental experiment.

The foregoing remarks, however, are not addressed to, nor can they be construed as an answer to the question "How ought one do moral philosophy?" or "What is the proper philosophical method?" But given the fact that one is interested in philosophy, they address the question of "How does one become one?" in a sense parallel to Kierkegaard's "How do I become a Christian?" This question is as much a retrospective as it is a prospective question. For one who has accomplished the philosophic task, the question will have merely a retrospective interest. But for one who is engaged in the process of becoming a philosopher, the question is a prospective one. And if philosophy, as Socrates taught and practiced, is in the end an enterprise in self-understanding, and self-understanding is a continuing task rather than an achievement, the question can only be a prospective one. The clarification of the question is inseparable from the content that is constitutive of the process of clarification. This is perhaps the reflexive character of philosophy as a struggle for self-knowledge. But in this sort of exploration, there is always the danger of self-deception. One needs to pay heed to Kierkegaard's remark: "It is one thing for a man to understand what he himself says, to understand himself in what he says is another thing."[16]

2

A Question of Moral Actuation

A. The Question of a Moral Agent

As a moral agent reflecting on the enterprise of moral thinking I propose a series of questions to a philospher of the moral life. One such
question may take the form: "What does your theory *mean* to me?" Is a
moral theory simply a piece of pure speculation or intellectual exercise
unrelated to my moral practice? If you have something to *tell* me, must
you allow that your theory is relevant to my life? If your answer is in
the affirmative and I am persuaded by the adequacy of your reasoning,
I still ask the question of how your theory is *possible* in practice. You
may claim special insights into the machinery of moral thinking and
action, but ultimately it is incumbent upon you to *show* me a way in
which your philosophical contributions can be an *active* force in living
problematic situations. At the very least, you must answer the question
of what may be termed *moral actuation,* i.e., the possibility of inspiring,
so to speak, your fine theoretical points with active properties. As an
agent I find it difficult to believe that moral inquiry is devoid of any
pragmatic aims or intentions. My question relates to this. If I am right
here, no philosopher, in the last analysis, can ignore the practical and
commitive character of his enterprise. Even Hume, who claims to be a
mere spectator of his moral practice, tells us that "the end of all moral
speculation is to teach us our duty."[1] Of course, the question is not
merely that of moral education, but of *moral dynamics*—the question of
producing a change in the present states of affairs by way of theoretical
reflection. It is a question of effectuating a body of moral commitments
within the life of moral agents. Admittedly this is more urgent for
practicing moralists than for philosophers. But a philosopher reflecting
upon this question, at least in the manner in which the agent's question
may be shown to be a problem or a question subject to a clear formulation, may illuminate the difficulties involved in this question. Perhaps,
while dealing with this question, the enterprise of moral theory may

change its character or focus, thus providing a much needed aid to the understanding of an aspect of the perplexities of serious moral agents. In the following sections we examine the various ways in which our hypothetical agent's question may be clarified and explore an answer to this question.

Some possible constructions of the question.   One way in which our agent's question may be clarified is an appeal to Kant's distinction between the principle of *discrimination* and the principle of *performance.* Discrimination concerns the measuring rod, performance is the mainspring of moral actions. "If we ask, 'What is morally good and what is not?' it is the principle of discrimination which is in question, in terms of which I decide the goodness of the action. But if we ask, 'What is it that moves me to act in accordance with the laws of morality?' we have a question which concerns the principle of the motive."[2]

The question posed by our hypothetical agent clearly lies in the principle of performance rather than discrimination. It is not a question of moral knowledge, of knowing the difference between right and wrong, or good and bad. That question already assumes the legitimacy and knowledge of moral distinctions; in other words, it does not concern a point in theory, but the actuation of any body of moral commitments, however it may be theoretically argued and supported. Surely our agent recognizes Kant's distinction and the gap between moral knowledge and action. The question of actuation is in part a problem of making moral principles and ideals moving forces in actual conduct. The question, "What sort of principle of performance is intrinsically related to the principle of discrimination?" as Kant envisages it, is a problem of moral motivation. How is actuation of the principle of discrimination possible? If we are to view the question as one of the psychology of motives, we still need to explain how these motives may be actuating forces in actual conduct. Unless motives can be shown to be in some way intrinsically related to our principle of discrimination, these motives would remain extrinsic to the practical obligatoriness of our moral knowledge. Even if the problem is seen as one of the psychology of moral motives, a principle of discrimination is still needed for proper and improper motives. We may appeal to our moral knowledge for this piece of discrimination. But does our moral knowledge by itself provide for this discrimination?

Moral knowledge, as consisting of a body of rules and principles, does not by itself provide the *rules* of application. If a moral rule is adjudged to be relevant to a particular situation, a judgment of relevance must be made. This judgment on the relevance of rules cannot be mapped out a priori, because of the contingent nature of moral situations. Actions as events occurring in the world do not appear with ready labels. If we are to apply moral labels to them, we must make judgments on the relevance of these labels. Our actions are then made to *suit* our words. But if we admit that some of our moral words are vague and open textured, and that situations may contain intrusive features not predetermined or anticipated by our moral rules, we must suit our words to actions themselves. We may need to make new labels or extend our old ones. If we stick to our old labels, our knowledge of a body of moral rules is, in Ryle's sense, bound to be purely *academic*. The question concerns the operative character of our academic knowledge, i.e., an operative knowledge in the sense of "the knowledge or conviction which manifests itself in the disposition to behave."[3] Moral knowledge in the operative sense is moral achievement. If moral achievement is possible, we must not merely have extrinsic motives, but an intrinsic moving plausibility of the academic moral knowledge itself.

Nor is our agent's question a *casuistical* one, in the sense of a question that calls for a systematic articulation of the practical import of the substance of an accepted moral practice. The success in giving a systematic clarification is a problem of casuistry, insofar as casuistry attempts to answer questions of application of moral rules to actual problematic situations. Moore rightly sees that ethics cannot be complete without casuistry.[4] Were we able to complete our casuistical investigations, the knowledge so arrived at would still remain hypothetical and academic for our moral agent. This sort of knowledge, of course, is a great aid to making moral judgments of the conduct of other agents. However, our agent seems to be asking a question of operative knowledge. If I know (academically) that certain actions are enjoined, forbidden, or permitted by the moral rules of my practice, this knowledge undoubtedly is a guide in my passing judgment upon the conduct of other agents or, for that matter, my own conduct. Casuistry can thus function in this retrospective fashion, in providing a guide to moral judgments by regarding actions as classifiable into various species. This sort of classification is again an academic one for the moral agent who is confronted by the problem of acting. As an actor, his knowledge, to be effective, must have a prospective character in action. The knowledge must be of the operative rather than the academic sort. If we grant the intrusive contingency of acting, casuistry, to be helpful, can be performed only from time to time, and only provisionally. In its clarificatory role, it is useful for moral education by prefiguring a framework upon which moral decisions may be made. The framework provides a sketch for a possible system of moral actions but does not contain any blueprints for preceptorial conformity in the flux of social and moral life.

Our agent's question cannot be construed as a question of casuistry or as a question of the psychology of motives. Perhaps we can learn something from a discussion of a theory of moral motivation. The question of actuation may, for instance, be viewed as a question of sanction. Bentham points out that "*sanctio,* in Latin, was used to signify the *act of binding,* and, by a common grammatical transition, anything which serves to bind a man: to wit, to the observance of such or such mode of conduct." According to this view, a sanction is "a source of obligatory powers or *motives:* that is, of *pains* and *pleasures;* which, according as they are connected with such or such modes of conduct, operate, and are indeed the only things which can operate, as *motives.*"[5] Thus Bentham cites physical, political, moral or popular, and religious sanctions in accounting for the binding force of his hedonistic utilitarianism. In this manner of regarding the problem of actuation, the philosopher's job is simply to point out the sorts of sanctions that are attendant upon the nonperformance of relevant moral obligations. Mill concurs here with Bentham: "The whole force of external reward and punishment, physical or moral, and whether proceeding from God or from fellow men, together with all the capacities of human nature admit of disinterested devotion to either, become available to enforce utilitarian morality, in proportion as that morality is recognized, and the more powerfully, the more the appliances of education and general cultivation are bent to this purpose."[6] So construed, our agent's question cannot be intelligible in terms of an intrinsic property of a moral doctrine; to be meaningful, it must be a question of moral strategy or tactics—of showing the devices that may be available as instruments of inducement of moral performance. In this sense, sanctions are rewards and punishments attendant upon action. Rewards are enticing devices, punishments repulsive ones. Admittedly these are techniques of inducement external to the intrinsic obligatoriness of moral rules. As philosophers we can point to these external aids to actuation rather than provide the moral agents with actuation that is somewhat intrinsic to our moral doctrine.

Mill realizes that Bentham's sanctions are external ones. External sanctions remain ineffectual agencies for actuating moral knowledge.

The question of the "binding force" of any supposed moral standard, which Mill regards, following Bentham, as a question of sanction or motive to obedience, is a proper question. "It arises, in fact, whenever a person is called on to *adopt* a standard, or refer morality to any basis on which he has not been accustomed to rest it."[7] Although Mill's interpretation of "binding force" in terms of sanction does not appear to answer our agent's question, it does point to the origin and importance of this question. On the face of it, the question may simply mean a question of self-interest: "What advantage may I, as an agent, derive in performing moral obligations?" It is not a question of sanction of pains and pleasures as Bentham viewed it, for the agent's pains and pleasures are not necessarily relevant to the question of the binding force of a moral doctrine. The construal of the question of actuation as a question of self-interest possibly lies beneath Shaftesbury's efforts at showing, for instance, "that to have the natural, kindly, or generous affections strong and powerful towards the good of the public, is to have the chief means and power of self-enjoyment [and] that to want them is certain misery and ill."[8]

The same view of the problem seems to lie at the heart of Butler's rather implausible insistence on the coincidence of benevolence and self-love. But our agent's question does not relate to his own interests. He is quite willing to grant the theoretical adequacy of any ethical doctrine. As Hume remarks: " 'What is that to me?' There are few occasions when this question is not pertinent."[9] The question is a *moral* one. As a moral agent, he lives within a moral practice that sometimes calls for the sacrifice of his own interests. He is not concerned with the question of justification, and thus the justification to self-interest is not the question here. The problem of actuation is not a problem of self-love, but a problem of the dynamics of any moral doctrine or knowledge. It concerns the *possibility* for any moral doctrine to be an intrinsically living and moving force in actual conduct without any appeal to extrinsic considerations. Although it may be quite true that the agent's interests are part of any moral considerations in practice, the question of interests is not the question of actuating moral knowledge.

Mill rightly sees that the question of the binding force of any supposed moral knowledge arises when a moral agent is considering whether he should adopt one doctrine rather than another. Our agent is a *moral* one in the sense that he is serious in playing the game of morality. He is questioning neither his moral practice nor any philosopher's doctrine in terms of validity. He is willing to play the moral game but is earnest in his quest for the dynamic force of moral knowledge intrinsic to his theoretical reflection. It is a question of adoption only in the sense that if a moral doctrine *cannot* provide its own dynamics in practice, this can constitute a possible ground for rejection. That Mill perhaps recognizes the importance of this sort of question is evidenced by his dissatisfaction with the doctrine of external sanctions. In his view, the *ultimate* sanction is an internal one—"a subjective feeling in our own minds . . . the conscientious feelings of mankind." It is "the desire to be in unity with our fellow creatures." Moreover, Mill takes note of the fact that "this sanction has no binding efficacy on those who do not possess the feelings it appeals to."[10] Thus Mill, like Hume, sees in the sentiment of humanity a special powerful force in activating our moral convictions. But our agent's question, if it can be tackled at all, is not a question of an appeal extrinsic to moral knowledge, but a question of an appeal intrinsic to it. An appeal to Mill's ultimate sanction still remains extrinsic to the nature of moral knowledge. If the term "ultimate" means "final or conclusive" the discussion of ultimate sanction remains an argument which, if sound, is a piece of academic knowledge. It argues to the practical possibility rather than accounting for the operative character of moral knowledge. The question is not simply one of converting, by various instrumental agencies, "a judgment of the understanding into a sentiment of the heart." The location of a special sort of feeling, even if it exists, cannot answer the question of our moral agent.

B. *Reformulation of the Question*

Although the preceding constructions of our agent's question do not provide satisfactory answers to the query, they do pertain to a more general problem of actuation. The discussion is useful in locating the general problem of which our agent's question may be regarded as a species. A clear delineation of our agent's question must be made from the more general problem, rather than by merely indicating what that question is *not*. We have already discussed the distinction between the *extrinsic* and *intrinsic* appeals of moral knowledge. This distinction points out the two facets of moral actuation. Even if the appeals to the casuistical import of moral doctrine, motivation, and more specifically sanctions of the internal and external variety are deemed to yield unsatisfactory answers to our moral agent's question, they remain actuating agencies of moral knowledge. The notion of actuation itself points to their relevance.

Although the notion of actuation does not find currency in philosophical writings, we may properly speak of actuating sentiment, passion, motives, or principles, as Hume has done in his moral inquiry.[11] We can also speak of a person as being actuated by interest, desire, or purpose. What is common to these items is the notion of a *moving* force in conduct. These various uses of actuation at the service of understanding human conduct are an interesting subject for exploration in the philosophy of action. They indicate ways in which the general problem of actuation may be dealt with. Insofar as a moral philospher is engaged in the descriptive-explanatory task, he may be concerned with sentiments, passions, principles, and motives that actuate the moral life of humanity. This is perhaps the major contribution of the Moral Sense School of the eighteenth century.

From the point of view of our agent's question in Section 2A, however, the various uses of the notion of actuation are extrinsic ways of coping with the problem of moral dynamics through the description and explanation of the moving forces of human conduct. In his question, it is the notion of *intrinsic* actuation of moral knowledge or doctrine that is central to his concern. His concern is not with a description and explanation of moral conduct but with the actuating possibility of the whole enterprise of morality. The issue is not one of the epistemology or psychology of morals, but of the actuating possibility of the whole character of moral inquiry. He wants an account of the dynamic force of moral philosophy of *any* persuasion. Extrinsic actuation helps delineate his question. Admitting the various uses of the notion of actuation, he wants the philosopher to offer an account of the intrinsic actuating possibility of any doctrine.

A philosopher may rejoin that our agent's question is one that does not admit of a philosophical answer. For the question in effect requires philosophical knowledge to have an intrinsic practical feature which is in fact extrinsic to the whole nature of philosophical enterprise. A philosopher has done his job so long as his thesis is supported by sound arguments, and in moral philosophy as long as he explains and illuminates the phenomena of the moral life. The realization of a philosopher's pragmatic and commitive aim cannot form part of its own argument. If a moral agent is perplexed in making his decision to adopt one theory rather than another, he must exercise a nonphilosophical choice. He must commit himself. He must learn to accept the gap between theoretical knowledge and practice. Each realm of activity, practical and theoretical, has an integrity of its own.

To our agent, on the other hand, the question of intrinsic actuation of moral knowledge is a real problem, especially when he is faced with the enterprise of moral theory which claims to offer insights—and at least in its traditional aim—to offer guidance to the moral life of humanity. How is this guidance in accordance with an ethical doctrine possible and plausible unless the ethical doctrine itself has an intrinsic feature of actuation? One cannot simply be content with the logical or empirical possibility of actuation through the utilization of extrinsic agencies in the education and cultivation of moral feelings, dispositions, and principles in the moral life. Moral knowledge, in the sense of being a product of inquiry, can only be academic knowledge, unless it can be shown to be intrinsically operative in conduct. To use the language of Kant, a principle of discrimination must, so to speak, contain within itself a principle of performance. We may now reformulate our agent's question: *How can a principle of discrimination be an actuating principle of performance without an appeal to matters extrinsic to the principle of discrimination itself?* The notion of "can" involved in the question is undoubtedly a difficult notion, for our agent wants a notion of possibility as an intrinsic possibility ingredient in the nature of moral knowledge itself.[12] If we take this question seriously, we need to show how a piece of academic knowledge can become an actuating force in human life. In other words, how can we establish the practical possibility of a piece of moral knowledge as a concrete feature in the life of a moral agent?

Kant and the problem of actuation.   In the chapter entitled "The Incentives of Pure Practical Reason" in the second critique, Kant appears to be struggling with the problem of actuation. Beck points out that "here Kant is concerned with an immanent phenomenological problem, not with one in the ontology of appearance and reality." The question is "How can a being in the phenomenal world, through his knowledge of the law of the intelligible, control his conduct so that this law does in fact become effective?"[13]

Kant remarks that the question of "how a law in itself can be the direct determining ground of the will (which is the essence of morality) is an insoluble problem for human reason." The question is identical with that of the possibility of human freedom. "Therefore, we shall not have to show a priori why moral law supplies an incentive but rather what it effects (or better, must effect) in the mind, so far as it is an incentive."[14]

In our terminology, Kant intends to give an a priori account for actuation in terms of the effect of moral law on the agent. This claim is interesting and significant, for it suggests the exclusion of extrinsic factors of actuation. Perhaps, like our hypothetical agent, Kant is here groping for a solution to the problem of intrinsic actuation. The incentive of pure practical reason, for him, lies in the feeling of respect—an effect of the agent's consciousness of the requirements of moral law. However, this account does not answer our agent's question: "How can practical knowledge have an actuating import without an appeal to extrinsic consideration?" For in this moral feeling of respect, we find no intrinsic actuating import of moral knowledge, but simply an effect consequent upon its actuating import. But in his discussion of moral incentives, Kant does throw light on our agent's question in seeing that moral actuation cannot be accounted for by factors extrinsic to moral law. In the *Foundations* he clearly states that "though respect is a feeling, it is not one received through any [outer] influence but is self-wrought by a rational concept."[15]

C. Exploration of an Answer

It is difficult to make our agent's question intelligible partly because of the general conception of knowledge that underlies the whole enterprise of moral theory. When philosophers appear to be concerned with the problem of actuation, for the most part they are dealing with factors that are extrinsic to their own doctrine. The root assumption here is the distinction between knowledge and action. To adopt Pepper's term, the *root metaphor* is, so to speak, the experienced radical disparity between thought and action.[16] More significantly, moral knowledge is construed as *anterior* rather than *posterior* to action. In this conception, although quite proper and important in the analytic understanding of the moral life, the knowledge in question is overtly or covertly propositional, or is based on the model of propositional knowledge. Thus the problem of actuation becomes, by and large, a problem in the psychology of moral agency. This conception of moral knowledge is unavoidable and may even be illuminating so long as we seek to explain the epistemic and psychological structure of moral action. It is an aid to locating the heart of the sort of actuation demanded by our moral agent.

In the sense of a conception of moral knowledge as *anterior* to action, when an item of knowledge assumes a practical character, i.e., when a moral rule or standard is conformed to, the action of conformity does not change the character of the rule itself. The nature of moral knowledge is not affected by actions that conform to it. In this view, actuation does not form part of the character of moral knowledge, since moral knowledge has its intrinsic features not affected by action. In considering the problem of actuation as formulated by our moral agent, we need a different view of moral knowledge. We need a notion of moral knowledge that is *posterior* rather than *anterior* to action. We need a notion of moral knowledge that contains within itself an intrinsic feature of actuation.

In order to take our agent's problem of actuation seriously, we introduce this notion of moral knowledge as *posterior* rather than anterior to actions. In this conception, we have an intrinsic actuating knowledge only when we have acted upon whatever *available* piece of academic moral knowledge we happen to possess. If a moral doctrine contains a set of rules and principles and ideals, there is a sense in which we *know* their significance and substantive constituents only when we have acted upon them. Thus the knowledge of the content of these principles, rules, and ideals depend on the actions performed rather than on our prior understanding of their practical import apart from actual moral performance. What gives an actuating force to a moral doctrine is, in effect, the *person* who embodies this doctrine in his conduct. It is thus the moral agent himself who actuates his academic moral convictions. The moral knowledge that is consequent and posterior to action has an intrinsic feature of actuation, not in an abstraction from moral performance, but as an ingredient in the moral performance itself. To speak of the intrinsic feature of moral knowledge in a person's life is to speak of an abstract distillation of an aspect or dimension of a moral life. To our agent we can explain that the difficulty of his question lies in the attempt to abstract a feature from the life of moral conduct. No definition of actuation can be given, for its meaning depends on the physiognomy of a moral life.[17] The agent has to recognize that feature of moral knowledge in his own performance. No conceptual account can be given of intrinsic actuation.

If our agent insists on a more specific answer to his question, we can perhaps point to certain persons as examples of actuating agencies without an appeal to the extrinsic factors of actuation which he rejects. We can say to him that in the moral life of different agents in diverse moral practices, certain persons have been regarded as paradigmatic for the actions of moral agents. These paradigmatic individuals, e.g., Jesus, Confucius, and Siddharta Gautama, are the grand actuating agencies of moral doctrines. In Jesus, for example, the ideal of love has become a real possibility—an ingredient possibility in the lives of some moral agents. The same is true of Confucius' *jên*, or ideal of humanheartedness, and Siddharta's *nirvana*. These paradigmatic individuals are not in themselves intrinsic actuators of moral knowledge, but they *exemplify* intrinsic actuation. We may therefore regard them as examples of intrinsic actuation. In pointing to these paradigmatic individuals in effect we focus on a concrete dimension of personal morality. We maintain a concrete perspective by seeing the manner in which academic moral knowledge is endowed with an actuating import.

If the heart of morality, as has been commonly maintained, requires the spirit of self-sacrifice, self-interested considerations and sanctions can at most amount to external agencies of actuation rather than intrinsically active ones. Actuating academic moral knowledge is, in Kantian terms, the union of the principles of discrimination and performance in persons, particularly the paradigmatic ones. Moral knowledge as *posterior* to action is moral *achievement*. If we choose to speak of "concrete realization of abstract knowledge" here, we must pay heed to the incomplete and progressive character of this sort of moral knowledge as moral achievement. If a paradigmatic individual like Confucius or Jesus can actuate moral principles and rules, these actuations in the life of ordinary moral agents are bound to affect the texture of prior knowledge by the sheer fact that these agents in their union of discrimination and performance bring to bear certain personal qualities of performance not previously determined by the character of the moral doctrine or moral practice.[18]

Hume glimpsed the actuating force of certain individuals, but it remained for him "something mysterious and inexplicable." He notes that "there is a *manner*, a grace, an ease, a genteelness, an I-know-notwhat, which some men possess above others, and which is very different from external beauty and comeliness, and which, however, catches our affection almost as suddenly and powerfully." But Hume rests content with pointing out that "this class of accomplishments . . . must be trusted entirely to the blind but sure testimony of taste and sentiment, and must be considered as a part of ethics left by nature to baffle all the pride of philosophy, and make her sensible of her narrow boundaries and slender acquisitions."[19] However, in putting a stress on the notion of paradigmatic individuals in our study and reflection on the moral life, we learn of an actuating agency for our moral theory. The philosophical significance of the notion of actuation lies in the moving away from the *mere abstract ways of speaking* about moral life to focus on a concrete dimension of the foundation of personal morality. A paradigmatic individual is not an example of a type, an illustration of an abstract piece of academic knowledge, but an exemplar of the actuating force of a moral doctrine. He is, for most moral agents with different cultural loci, unique and authoritative in his own way. In philosophy we have our own paradigmatic individuals too. As Hampshire insightfully remarks, "As with Moore, so also with Austin, there was a tendency among those who felt his authority to turn his individual style of thought into a general method of solving problems. There is always this desire to make any outstanding individual a type. The distinction and individuality are then reduced to manageable and imitable proportions. But the results of such a reduction of an individual style to a general method are often trivialities."[20]

May we not say the same thing to our moral agent? His question is a serious one. He is in search of a paradigmatic individual as an actuating force for what he regards as academic knowledge. We are unable to give him the account of intrinsic actuation that he wants. But we can point to the examples of paradigmatic individuals in the hope of easing his perplexity. In this manner, we also learn that moral knowledge as posterior to action is a moral achievement. A philosopher can only point to the importance of the notion of paradigmatic individuals as furnishing examples of actuating agency for moral knowledge. He cannot himself provide the actuation intrinsic to his moral inquiry. The moral agent has to answer that question of actuation himself. In pointing out the character of actuation in paradigmatic individuals, perhaps the philosopher has completed his task. How this task may be further developed remains an interesting question to explore. For the conception of moral knowledge as moral achievement is in need of a systematic explication. But this task should not affect the relevance of this notion to our agent's problem of actuation.

D. *The Import of the Question of Intrinsic Actuation*

If the foregoing attempt at making intelligible the question of moral actuation is deemed to be a successful experiment in understanding an aspect of moral agency, we still need to inquire into the motivation for and the import of the question to both moral theory and practice. The *assumption* underlying the question, if regarded as both intelligible and reasonable, tells much about the sort of demands the agent places on his moral practice and moral theory in general. The assumption lies in a legitimate demand upon moral theory and practice to exhibit some sort of *transforming significance* in the life of a reflective agent. This may be better appreciated in extreme situations of anguish and perhaps pathological perplexities that beset some moral agents who contemplate suicide. As Schopenhauer insightfully remarked, "Suicide [aside from great mental suffering] may also be regarded as an experiment which man puts to Nature, trying to force her to answer. The question is this: What *change* will death produce in a man's existence and his insight into the nature of things? It is a clumsy experiment to make, for it involves the destruction of the very consciousness which puts the question and awaits the answer."[21] Of course, this demand and quest need not, in ordinary reflective agents, take this pathological form. The agent's perplexity speaks out for a transforming significance of the whole intellectual and moral being of his psyche in search for a meaning in his life and death. The question of the meaning of death, for instance, is in part the question "How does a conception of death transform the person's life?" Kierkegaard justly said,

> If the answer to our question is affirmative [i.e., we can apprehend death by means of any conception of it] the question then arises as to what death is, and especially as to what it is for the living individual. We wish to know how the conception of death will *transform a man's entire life,* when in order to think its uncertainty he has to think it in every moment, so as to prepare himself for it. We wish to know what it means to prepare for death. . . . The question must be raised of the possibility of finding an ethical expression for the significance of death; and a religious expression for the victory over death; one needs a solving word which explains its mystery, and a binding word by which the living individual defends himself against the ever recurrent conception; for surely we dare scarcely recommend mere thoughtlessness and forgetfulness as wisdom.[22]

As we shall see in later chapters, the question of meaning in one's life is tied to the quest for ideals and styles of life, to the achievement of self-respect and dignity of persons. For the present, let us confine our attention to the question of intrinsic actuation in relation to moral theory and practice. Regarding the former relation, a moral theory, whether deontological or teleological, does impose certain obligations upon the moral agents who are committed to it. The import of our question lies in the demand upon the transforming significance of a normative theory on the life of moral agents in general. This is not to be confused, as suggested in Section 2A, with the question of application of theory to practice or with the question of strategies or instrumentalities necessary in implementing any theory in question. It is not claimed here that a moral theory cannot stand on its own or be *understood* in the abstract sense of understanding its structure, internal coherence, and implications for actual practice. In this regard, the enterprise of moral theory does not depend upon the actual fulfillment of its normative demands. Its adequacy, as Kant points out, does not depend upon concrete moral performance.

Moreover, a moral theory can profit much from a reflection upon this question, for if it takes the question of intrinsic actuation seriously, it can attend to the possibility of its dynamic power and influence in practice. Although it cannot provide an answer to this question, it can explore the possibility of paradigms in persons who embody the theory in their lives and conduct. A philosophical exploration of paradigmatic individuals may not provide a necessary factor in a moral agent's process of commitment to a theory or in the agent's envisagement of a way or a style of life. A focus on the significance and function of paradigmatic individuals in various moral practices, however, does point to these persons as a sort of "catalyst" for the agent's imagination in considering concrete presentations of ways and styles of life. Thus a focus on paradigmatic individuals can be causally valuable and highly efficacious in the reflective agent's valuative process. In a sense, the intrinsic actuating capability of paradigmatic individuals might be compared to an inductive process in electricity. Such individuals are the forces that move by inducing intrinsic actuating force in the reflective moral agent. In this way, the paradigmatic individuals who exemplify the actuation of the theory can provide examples of actuation which may well be a main constitutive base for the practical understanding of a moral theory from the point of view of a reflective moral agent.

Thus a distinction should be made between theoretical and practical understanding of a moral theory. Moral theories can be expounded, justified, and explained apart from the question of intrinsic actuation. This intellectual process is familiar to teachers and students of ethics. The dialectical interplay of arguments and interest in live issues in our communal life can yield a good measure of understanding of our moral life by way of clarification of moral concepts, arguments, and procedures for assessing diverse moral claims. Moreover, if we attend to the question of intrinsic actuation, commonly phrased in terms of the vague question of relevance, we can appreciate the force of this question as primarily prompted by a desire to learn the transforming significance of a moral theory. The question the teacher confronts may not be of the form "How adequate is a utilitarian theory?" or "How can a utilitarian theory, of any appropriate version, solve our urgent moral issues in contemporary society?" but rather "How do I *become* a utilitarian?" in the parallel sense in which Kierkegaard inquires "How do I become a Christian?" in his *Concluding Unscientific Postscript.* It is then the question of the task of becoming subjective, of achieving some sort of personal transformation in light of utilitarian theory.

If we recognize the legitimacy of this quest, as teachers of ethics, we must take the question seriously and perhaps address ourselves to the provision of paradigms for application as exemplification of the theory in question. Here is not a question of vivid dramatic presentation, but of appreciative response to the question, thereby providing aids in practical understanding of moral theory. In this way, the paradigmatic individuals studied can have an integral role to play in the practical understanding of moral theories in general. It may also be of profit to point out to the moral agent in quest of intrinsic actuation that a successful quest can furnish a vital source for moral creativity. The task of moral creativity, as I see it, can receive light from an inquiry into the nature and function of paradigmatic individuals within a moral practice. The following three chapters are devoted to this task. I hope to show what sort of relation is possible between a moral practice and its paradigmatic exemplars, and its significance for our problem of moral creativity.

3

Morality and the Paradigmatic Individuals

A. Creative Moral Pioneers

In *The Language of Morals,* Hare maintains that it is in practice impossible to specify completely a way of life in which a person's decisions of principle form a part. We are told that "the nearest attempts are those given by the great religions, especially those which can point to historical persons who carried out the way of life in practice."[1] This emphasis on the importance of historical persons gains significance in a man's moral life only when they are in some manner viewed as living exemplars of conduct. Thus in Chapters 4 and 5 I attempt to exhibit this role in Confucian ethics.

Nielsen recently suggested that "for the most part, people get their standards not from ethical treatises or even scriptural texts or homely sayings, but by idealizing and following the examples of some living person or persons."[2] If this suggestion is sound, it points to the view that in some fashion, certain persons are a source of actual conduct for moral agents. A study of some founders of living religions may help us determine how they enter into the lives of moral agents in various moral practices. This interesting study has been carried out in Jaspers' exposition of Socrates, Siddharta Gautama, Confucius, and Jesus as four paradigmatic individuals who have "exerted a historical influence of incomparable scope and depth." Jaspers states that "no single type can account for these four," for "their historicity and consequent uniqueness can be perceived only within the all embracing historicity of humanity, which each of them expresses itself in a wholly different way" (p. 3).[3] The present chapter centers on the theme of paradigmatic individuals as creative moral agents and as having a significant import in moral practice of ordinary agents committed to the actuating force of the paradigms.

Jaspers notes that Socrates, Buddha, Confucius, and Jesus "became models for mankind without setting themselves up as examples" (p. 95). Each of them appears as a unit class, but also as a model that is exemplary in some way. An exemplar is not literally an example, otherwise it would be an example of a type. It is more like a Goethean *genuine symbol*—"a particular instance which is coalescent with a universal and which thereby plays a unique role by revealing, in a way which no particular could quite do, the nature of that more general something."[4] And yet it cannot be a particular instance of a type, but a particular that functions in some universal or paradigmatic way. The term *model* as applied to these individuals is also misleading, for it suggests something to imitate. Although it is possible to imitate the conduct of these historical persons, imitation does not necessarily portray the spirit which appears to be embodied in the lives of these persons.

How then can a particular person function as a paradigmatic individual?   Every living person is placed in a *historic situation.* He lives within the orbit of his cultural inheritance in the face of a changing environment. In the midst of a moral crisis, he must decide whether his encounter with the cultural tradition inherent in his moral practice will take the form of rejection or critical acceptance. To reject the tradition *in toto* is to cut oneself off from one's historic roots. It is in a sense to lose one's personhood, for one loses the anchor of identification. The use of language is by itself an indication of our historic roots. Wittgenstein says, "To imagine a language means to imagine a form of life." Speech is "part of an activity, or of a form of life."[5] Language, as a form of life, embodies a tradition that furnishes the source from which our activities may gain a practical import. Moral discourse, in particular, reflects certain preestablished standards and criteria for assessing conduct. To claim an absolute separation from the tradition without the use of language is to remain silent. Socrates, Buddha, Confucius, and Jesus undoubtedly have their moments of silence, of reflection on their own predicaments. But they do speak against the backgrounds of their situations. In so doing, however partially, they must acknowledge their historic reality.

Speech, moreover, is not an indication of mere acceptance, for each manner of speaking is a *style of orientation* to a tradition. It may be an act of critical acceptance, as in the case of Socrates in *Crito,* or an act of critical transformation, as in the case of Confucius. It may also be an act of acceptance in order to achieve transcendence from existential predicaments, as in the cases of Jesus and Buddha. The uniqueness of these men appears to lie in their peculiar *styles*.

In his manner of relating himself to a tradition, the paradigmatic individual in effect transfuses the content of the tradition into his own life. The effect is one of transfiguration. Herein lies the supreme venture—the risk of disapproval and condemnation of his fellow beings. This is perhaps the reason why the paradigmatic individuals can inspire devotion and enthusiasm and at the same time evoke hostile response from their audience. Transfiguration can be achieved only after a struggle. Once it is achieved, its novelty and suasive power become accepted by the majority. It may become the source of a new tradition, but in itself—in a living person—it is not a tradition. This may account for the fact that the lives of the paradigmatic individuals cannot really be our own. As Jaspers remarks, "In general, the content of their thinking cannot be ours, but their manner of thinking can show us the way" (p. 96). However, the paradigmatic individual may be a source upon which my life may build, but my life may also crumble thereby, for the source is hollow, the style cannot be my own. As Alcibiades said of Socrates, "I don't know whether anybody else has ever opened him up when he's being serious, and seen the little images inside, but I saw them once, and they looked so godlike, so golden, so beautifully and so utterly amazing that there was nothing for it but to do exactly what he told me."[6] What makes these images significant is precisely the *transhistorical possibilities* that seem to be suggested by the paradigm. Although the paradigm is situated in a historic present, it seems to *project* itself in a prospective historical future. In this sense, each may be viewed as a Leibnizean monad pregnant with possibilities. These future possibilities, in order to be significant to any person, have to be individuated. In this individuating concreting process, the paradigm may function, on the one hand, as a source of retrospective justification for moral agents, and on the other hand, as a prospective task to be accomplished. From the retrospective point of view, the paradigmatic individual is an embodiment of a set of moral principles and rules that an agent may appeal to for justification of his acts. From the prospective point of view, the paradigmatic individual is an embodiment of moral ideals which sets the task for personal moral accomplishment. Since paradigmatic individuals like Confucius, Jesus, Buddha, and Socrates are a source of morality, living in the knowledge of this source and living in accordance with a tradition is an achievement.

We may note that with the possible exception of Jesus, none of the individuals mentioned claimed himself to be paradigmatic. Socrates was a man in earnest quest for self-knowledge compatible with his view of man's characteristic rationality. Confucius was a man who hoped to reinstitute an ideal of a harmonious social order which he thought to be implicit in the Chou dynasty. Buddha bowed in silence regarding his own liberation from the wheel of *samsara*. Socrates did not proclaim the success of his quest. In accordance with our knowledge drawn from the *Analects*, Confucius never asserted himself as being in any way paradigmatic. Each lived his life as a moral pioneer within an established tradition. The success of their pioneering tasks is a testimony to their moral genius.

How do the four paradigmatic individuals acquire their historic significance and moral relevance?   All four were moral pioneers or reformers. From the point of view of the psychology of personality, they are in Max Weber's sense *charismatic* persons, possessing, in the eyes of their followers, a set of unusually attractive qualities or powers of moral leadership, a sense of devotion to a mission and confidence in its rightness, and also an ability to display these qualities in concrete situations of doing and suffering. Charisma is "always alien to the world of everyday routine: it calls for new ways of life and thought."[7] This accounts for the innovative and revolutionary character of these men. From the point of view of the content of their teachings, their utterances have two prominent characteristics. First, the moral principles and ideals which they espoused and preached are vague, for the principles and ideals announced do not completely specify the rules or types of acts falling within a well-defined scope of application, nor do they spell out the criteria for determining the appropriate situations to which the principles are intended to apply. Room is thus left for individual interpretation and decision. Second, the same utterances adjudged by posterity to be vague appear to have their suggestive and persuasive relevance to concrete situations of human concern. The vagueness of the sayings of Jesus, Confucius, Buddha, and Socrates owes much to the viewpoint of posterity; to their disciples the masters' remarks might have appeared to have a crystal clarity. Their spoken words had perhaps an imperative and directive force. Their immediate clarity derived from their felicity and relevance to actual situations. To their audience, the spoken words seemed to solve the hearers' problems. The success of these remarks terminates as soon as the problematic situations become unproblematic ones. At the same time these solutions acquire a universal function.

The insight of these moral pioneers lies in their reflective view of the human predicament to be met with by every moral agent. Since the predicament is a universal one, insightful solutions that liberate moral agents from the predicament will acquire relevance in moral conduct. The forceful relevance of the utterances of the paradigmatic individuals bears on their capacity to relate themselves to existential moral crises by way of providing a new style or way of life in which a living person may organize his own ideals and aspirations. The insights may then become universalized rules for later generations. But for any paradigmatic insight to retain its dynamic and persuasive force, it cannot be encapsulated in a book of rules and precepts to be followed and obeyed but must be a set of guidelines that acquires regulative authority through the practical test of its capacity to bear continuing relevance to concrete problems of deliberation and choice. In the words of Aristotle, "In the field of moral action truth is judged by the actual facts of life, for it is in them that the decisive element lies."[8]

It is one thing to express appreciation for the power of a paradigmatic individual and another to view him as a regulative source of a moral practice. We may appreciate a paradigm because of its suasive powers and personal qualities that command respect and admiration, but the application of the paradigm's utterances compels us to recognize the paradigm as a source of moral practice, as generative of particular solutions to particular problems. Viewing the paradigms apart from their original homes, they become universal symbols of striving for Buddhistic *nirvana,* Christian union with God, Socratic self-illumination, and Confucian cosmic harmony. With a little less detachment from their historic loci, the symbols are transformed into images of insight into particular living situations. As symbols the paradigms tend to float in the realm of abstraction or ideality. As images they find the concrete locus that gives them life.

In a sense the continuing relevance of a paradigmatic individual in the life of a moral agent is a progressive articulation of its relevance to the agent's problem of choice and decision. When the moral principles learned from paradigmatic persons are assented to and adopted by a moral agent, these principles may then function as promissory notes to be reckoned with, leaving, however, the terms of fulfillment to the appropriate circumstance of individual judgment and decision. In this way, a moral agent can also be paradigmatic in a more modest way, in the manner in which he exercises his judgment of application of principles. The judgments are in effect his rulings on the relevance of the paradigms, even though by his actions he may not succeed in a scope of influence comparable to that of the four paradigmatic individuals. His judgments and corresponding actions may not be universal, and consequently may have a restricted scope of relevance to other persons.

What then accounts for the universality of function in the paradigmatic individuals? The difficulty of answering this question lies in the problem of describing the paradigmatic individuals. If we grant that each of the four is *unique* in some way, their uniqueness seems to be an elusive thing. It seems to escape any attempt at an adequate description, for any description imports criteria that are foreign to the life of the person. In addition to this difficulty, in relating the lives of these paradigms, our description cannot be easily distinguished from our evaluation. As Warnock recently pointed out, ordinary discourse neither is nor needs to be regimented, like legal proceedings. If I am telling someone, for instance, "about the career of Mussolini, it would be unrealistic to look for—to assume that there must be—a point at which description of his doings terminates, and evaluation of them begins." This is, of course, not a claim that the distinction between description and evaluation cannot be made, but a claim that in ordinary discourse "one might expect to find description and evaluation so inextricably intermingled as to constitute, as it were, a seamless garment."[9]

To distinguish paradigmatic individuals from ordinary men, I propose that we say that the former as paradigms *generate* their own criteria for evaluation. Their uniqueness lies in their *styles of life* rather than in their content. The language of criteria has, so to speak, a retrospective significance from the point of view of a moral agent. Bits and pieces of speech and conduct thus function as criteria only *ex post facto*, and then only to other men.

The notion of "generation of criteria" is more than just a metaphor. It is used to capture the living significance of the paradigmatic individuals. The term is used to focus on the *creativity* of a moral life that prospectively functions as an embodied set of criteria for other people, and retrospectively functions as a source of justification. Both the prospective and the retrospective uses of a paradigm are attempts at a sort of description from the point of view of their regulative significance to a moral agent. Each paradigm seems to exemplify in his life a set of criteria for evaluating conduct, but such exemplifications amount to a way of speaking that stresses the *universality* of function of a particular person. As a particular *qua* particular, the criteria viewed by moral agents as implicit in the paradigms are in reality extrinsic to the lives of these paradigmatic individuals. In other words, a particular person acquires paradigmatic authority by virtue of its cognitive and persuasive relevance to the living problems of the moral agents. Of itself a particular individual cannot endow with any effectiveness its own universality, for there are, strictly speaking, no self-authenticating acts of any individual. A self-appointed paradigm can at most be a possibility of a paradigm. Being a paradigm is an appreciation and recognition by others. It is a recognition of a living spirit in a moral history. No self-authenticating act is ultimately possible, from the point of view of rational persuasion, without backing from an external source, whether divine revelation, established historical authority, or political and social sanctions. But none of these can have any force without an act of ascription by others.

Thus an individual, without his authority being assented to by others, cannot pronounce his own utterances as authoritative. He has to present legitimate credentials for his authority to be recognized. Uniqueness of moral creativity is a style that is at the same time an achievement. The uniqueness of a style of life is not a given but an accomplished fact. If the notion of a moral agent is to be construed as a unique person that admits, according to Kant, of neither market nor fancy price, it is because the dignity of persons is an award, not an intrinsic characteristic of human beings *qua* human beings. Since we do not award uniqueness to everyone, we must have some grounds for doing so. (This will be discussed further in Chapter 7.) Paradoxically, the uniqueness of the paradigmatic individuals consists by and large in the criteria that they project and sometimes articulate for their followers and posterity, for they generate their own criteria. They bespeak their own norms of conduct that serve as guides for others. From our own point of view as moral agents, the criteria must function consistently in their various and varying applications. But this consistency, as recognized in recent moral philosophy, is a requirement of rationality, but not a requirement of a paradigmatic life. The larger sense of consistency is at stake here—a consistency that is fitting and appropriate. It is the consistency of a rhythm of life, of an ongoing process of conduct throughout a man's life, not that of one proposition with another.

The claim that I am different from other men is not an announcement of my uniqueness as a person. Descriptively, the focal difference lies in the biocultural space that is occupied by a man as a living organism. To point to this difference is to point to a distinction that need not be a mark of *distinction*. The ambiguity of the notion of distinction moves between the descriptive and the normative. Uniqueness is a difference that is normatively distinctive. It is a normative notion of merit. Being uniquely paradigmatic as a person is an endowment or entitlement given by others by virtue of the fact that the person in question possesses certain qualities judged to be meritorious on certain acknowledged criteria. Although a person cannot authenticate his utterances or actions with any effectiveness, he can present grounds for such an authentication by others. He can present merit claims, but these claims still have to be assessed before their authority can be acknowledged. The notion of the dignity and worth of a person is a dubious notion if it is intended as a way of asserting the intrinsic property of being a person. Moreover, the use of this notion has a persuasive force, for in a democratic society it is an effective weapon against the oppression of individual liberty. Neither the belief in nor the exercise of liberty assures us of any recognized merit as a person, but it does point to the importance of social provision of opportunities for individuals to acquire merits.

The four paradigmatic individuals are the living foundations of personal moralities. They are sources of principles and ideals, and they support certain continuing moral practices. The uniqueness of their styles, their manners of organizing their lives, have been an inspirational source of moral guidance. This at any rate has been true of the majority of moral agents in these moral practices. The significance of the notion of paradigmatic individuals thus lies in its focus upon *a* foundation of personal morality in terms of its historic and dynamic source rather than in terms of an abstract model of reason and sentiment. Like the paradigmatic individuals, a moral agent also lives within a given moral tradition. He must exercise his judgment concerning the significance of the ideals and principles implicit in his moral practice. His *practical wisdom* consists in his ability to mold the existing tradition into his own style of life—an organized pattern of living that gives meaning to his aspirations and values. From his point of view, a paradigmatic individual stands as a preeminent exemplar of excellence and virtue, for the paradigm provides a source of both moral principles and values. The rules and principles that a paradigm embodies are an agent's articulation of the principal features of a life with a style of its own. In the same sort of way, the moral agent carries within himself the burden of a tradition—a continuing burden to make the moral practice, originally inspired and founded by the paradigm, relevant to *his* problems and to the common predicament of humanity. The *spirit* of the paradigm is the spirit of moral creativity within a moral practice. A historic source of a moral practice, in this way, gives room also to emergent personal novelties.

In the paradigmatic individuals, reason and sentiment are not distinct, words and actions do not form an articulate inference. Principles and actions are not placed in a logical map. The paradigm, detached from its life, may serve as a map with a set of principles of morality that function as vessels to be filled rather than substance to be ingested. Since their words and actions are responses to the problematic situations which they encountered, these words and actions cannot literally be our own. Their particular insights and seeming appropriateness of conduct are tied to their historicity. We, as moral agents, still need to locate the fittingness of these insights within our own psychological, social, and cultural milieu. Our creativity thus consists in our ability to give the principles implicit in our moral practice a meaningful content. We also act in accordance with them with a style of our own. We may not be paradigmatic in the same sense as were Socrates, Confucius, Jesus, and Buddha, but some of our actions when fitting and appropriate to living situations may be paradigmatic for others, for our children, friends, and acquaintances. And in extending the scope of our activities and concern for others, some of our actions may be paradigmatic even for persons who may not have any special relation to us. This is perhaps the point of Chang Tsai's advice: "In one's words there should be something to teach others, . . . in one's activities there should be something to serve as a model for others."[10] As a source of value our paradigm is an ideal to which we aspire. In acting in consonance with an ideal we may also generate ideals for others.

Thus from the point of view of a moral agent, behind his living moral practice or tradition, there are paradigmatic individuals that form his inspiration and sustain his life. However, since the content of these individuals' lives cannot be our own, there is still room for moral creativity of agents within a moral practice. As Jaspers succinctly remarks, the paradigmatic individuals are the "beacons by which to gain an orientation, not models to imitate" (p. 96). They furnish us a model for understanding moral creativity in relation to moral practices in general. After a brief historical digression, we shall return to a discussion of their actuating and standard-guiding role in moral practices.

For convenience, we shall henceforth use PI as an abbreviation for Paradigmatic Individual(s).

B. *Some Historical Observations*

The notion of a PI, i.e., a particular entity functioning as a universal, is not without an interesting historical anticipation. In Berkeley's *Treatise Concerning the Principles of Human Knowledge,* there are two familiar passages that appear to suggest the notion of PI:

> An idea, which considered in itself is particular, becomes general by being made to represent or stand for all other particular ideas of the same sort. To make this plain by an example, suppose a geometrician is demonstrating the method of cutting a line in two equal parts. He draws, for instance, a black line of an inch in length, this which in itself is a particular line is nevertheless with regard to its signification general, since as it is there used, it represents all particular lines whatsoever; for that which is demonstrated of it, is demonstrated of all lines whatsoever; or, in other words, of a line in general.

> *Universality,* so far as I can comprehend not consisting in the absolute, positive nature or conception of anything, but in the relation it bears to the particulars signified or represented by it: by virtue whereof it is that things, names or notions, being in their own nature *particular,* are rendered universal.[11]

These two passages suggest the interpretation that particular things, names, or notions can function as paradigms. Universality, on this view, is the function of a particular. The particular, so to speak, functions as a representative individual of a class. Devoid of its representative or paradigmatic function, it can of course be regarded as a mere member of a class, or as an example of a class of objects possessing a specifiable set of properties. Whether or not Berkeley has succeeded in solving the problem of universals, his incisive remarks can serve as a contribution to the understanding of the notion of PI. Our interest here, of course, relates primarily to its use in the discussion of moral creativity.

However, a question may be properly raised: If a particular is to function in a representative or universal capacity, how does one explain the notion of resemblance that seems to underlie Berkeley's view? One may ask, if the notion of resemblance is to be employed, are we to take resembling particulars as a natural or purely conventional matter, i.e., as dependent on a conceptual system of classification? In the First Draft to the Introduction to the *Principles* Berkeley remarks that "these sorts [of likeness] are not determined and set out by Nature, as was thought by most philosophers. Nor yet are they limited by any precise, abstract ideas settled in the mind, with the general name annexed to them as is the opinion of the author of the Essay [Locke], nor do they in truth, seem to me to have any precise bounds or limits at all."[12] This remark would seem to deny the alternative views implied by our question. In Berkeley's view, in principle, there are no precise restrictions in the use of particulars as paradigms. It is possible to speculate here that perhaps he is groping for a performative view of this sort. The universality of the function of a particular sign, object, or for that matter person constitutes the epistemic criterion for resemblance, but this does not imply that it is a determinate criterion in the sense of being a criterion for classification. The classificatory *use* of the paradigm is not denied. It depends on our interest and our decision within proper contexts of inquiry. In the way in which the use is acknowledged to have a force in our inquiry, it does not function as an arbitrary convention. Occurrent resemblance need not be denied on this view, for the question of what is to be regarded as a PI depends ultimately upon our decision of selectivity following on our notion of what is or what is not important in the context of our interest. In effect, the sort of view we are speculating upon, apart from its possible relevance to the problem of universals, may be called a performative thesis. On this view, we *make* use of a particular to function in a universal way. The use depends on the context of discourse. The PI is strictly not a criterion, but it can function, particularly in the case of persons, as a standard of some sort.

The preceding remarks ascribe credit to Berkeley's insight without the intention of making it a solution to the difficult philosophical problem of universals. We merely acknowledge Berkeley's contribution and its importance to moral inquiry.

In moral theory, the importance of the notion of PI has long been recognized, though it does not play a central role. In the *Nicomachean Ethics,* Aristotle suggests that a man of high moral standard can function as a measure of conduct. In the context of the discussion on wish as concerned with the end, he suggests that "what seems good to a man of high moral standards is truly the object of wish" rather than the wish of a worthless man. In moral questions, "a man whose standards are high judges correctly, and in each case what is truly good will appear to him to be so." His chief distinction lies "in his ability to see the truth in each particular moral question, since he is, as it were, the standard and measure for such questions" (1113a). In another passage, Aristotle suggests that it is not by individual choice of the end, but "by a natural gift of vision, as it were, which enables him to make correct judgments and choose what is truly good: to be well-endowed by nature means to have this natural gift" (1114b).

To Aristotle, then, living PIs are important to moral agents since they seem to possess in some way a sort of vision and keen perception of the significance of particular situations. Their lives and conduct exemplify the embodiment of this vision which can serve as a standard for ordinary moral agents. We shall discuss the nature of this standard-guiding function in Section 3C.

Since Aristotle, moral philosophers paid little attention to the importance of the notion of PI until Bergson's *Two Sources of Morality and Religion*. Bergson distinguishes two moralities: the morality of obligation or pressure and the morality of aspiration. The morality of obligation is the "representation of a society which aims at self-preservation. . . . The feeling which would characterize the consciousness of these pure obligations assuming they were all fulfilled, would be a state of individual and social well-being similar to that which accompanies the normal working of life. It would resemble pleasure rather than joy." The morality of aspiration, on the other hand, "implicitly contains the feeling of progress," the feeling of an enthusiasm of a forward movement that spreads over the world.[13] This latter morality is the morality of PIs, the "founders and reformers of religions, mystics and saints, obscure heroes of moral life whom we have met on our own way and who are in our eyes the equal of the greatest, they are all there: inspired by their example, we follow them, as if we were joining an army of conquerors."[14] For the most part, Bergson seems to think of PIs simply as examples or representations of what is best in us, rather than ascribing to them a standard-guiding function. Moreover, he has the keen insight that it is these exceptional men who transformed the morality of closed society to that of open society or of extensive love. One would want more explication of the notion of PI. We should also observe in this connection that Bergson appears to be more concerned with the emotive response of moral agents to the PIs than the function of PIs in relation to the morality of obligation. The stress on the enthusiasm of the follower seems relevant to the psychology of responding to PIs rather than an elucidation of their nature. Bergson thinks that the enthusiasm is one of love of humanity. But this seems to import a normative criterion into the notion of

PI. In view of the problem of translation of moral appraisive concepts from one language to another, as forcefully shown by Aschenbrenner's *Concepts of Values,* it appears to be arbitrary to erect a normative criterion as a criterion of understanding moral practices. As we shall see later, the concept of *jên,* as in Confucian ethics, cannot be rendered arbitrarily as "benevolence" or "love of humanity" without a careful qualification of the sorts of contexts acknowledged within the Confucian moral practice. It is also doubtful whether the concept of love can be unequivocally ascribed to Buddhistic moral practice. This observation, of course, does not diminish Bergson's insight into the dynamics of morality in terms of his morality of aspiration.

C. Actuation and the Standard-Guiding Function

After the brief historical digression we should now turn our attention to the actuating role of PIs and their standard-guiding function. In the interest of an epistemology of morals, one may properly question the evaluation of PIs. In Section 3A I suggested that there are no self-authenticating acts of a person for being a PI. A proper answer to the question of evaluation lies in the recognized rules and principles embedded in particular moral practices. This is not to deny that a philosopher should attempt to formulate rational criteria for the assessment of persons acknowledged as PIs by the moral agents of various moral practices. It should be noted, however, that if the question of intrinsic actuation is regarded as meaningful and important, the moral agent finally must assess himself. As Nicolai Hartmann points out, "The satisfaction which a model [in the sense of PI] gives its very quality of being a pattern consists in its agreement with standards which I consciously or unconsciously apply. The setting up of a person as a pattern is already a moral judgment upon the person as a value. The choice takes place from the valuational points of view."[15] These standards external to PIs' functions may be purely personal or standards having some sort of tie with a moral practice. Such standards, moreover, provide a normative identification for the agent's moral beliefs or commitments, for if his commitments are totally alien to the moral practice, his use of moral concepts in the articulation of his commitments would be totally deprived of a meaningful frame of reference and import. He may have an idiosyncratic moral vocabulary quite foreign to that current in the discourse of ordinary moral agents living in the same community.

At this juncture, it is perhaps worthwhile to clarify further the dis-

tinction between personal models and paradigms, which was used intu-
itively in Section 3A. We have avoided the use of "personal model"
since this notion suggests unthinking imitation of the lives and conduct
of certain persons without regard to moral criteria. This is not to deny
that certain persons within a moral practice can function as models of
emulation. This distinction between persons as models and persons as
PIs can perhaps be better elucidated in terms of the distinction between
standards of aspiration and standards of inspiration. Both these sorts
of standard can have a guiding function. A moral standard of aspiration typically sets the target of high moral achievement, but what the
agent takes as a standard in this sense depends largely upon his levels
of aspiration. A personal model, functioning as an aspirational standard, would be a static telos or target for imitation rather than a beacon
of moral creativity. As Horsburgh remarked, few moral agents "aspire
without being inspired; and only that which seems to admit of moral
improvement, which can be entirely accepted and approved, is able to
inspire us."[16] However, a person, a PI functioning as a standard of
inspiration, does not specify the level of aspiration. What a PI provides
is a point of orientation, not a task intellectually conceived and articulated, but a task that is *being* conceived or being formed in the process
of doing. In having a PI as a standard of inspiration, the moral agent in
effect defines the content of such an inspiration. In this sense he becomes clearer about his task by developing the point of orientation in
conjunction with his moral attitudes and performance. As I shall suggest in Chapter 8, there is a sense in which moral ideals function as
points of orientation as distinct from those that function as policies of
ways of life.

Although I have suggested that criteria for assessment of the PIs
depend on criteria acknowledged as integral to particular moral practices, we can learn from a study of the four PIs Socrates, Jesus, Siddharta, and Confucius. The rationale for our acceptance of these PIs as
standards of inspiration appears to lie in their distinctive embodiment
of ideal excellence variously conceived and interpreted in different
moral practices. An ideal of excellence, conceived of as a supreme telos,
whether of justice and virtue, Christian charity, compassion, or *jên*
(human-heartedness), is in some fashion viewed as embodied and particularized in the lives of these persons. Lesser paradigms are perhaps
more the embodiment of particular virtues or excellences. Or they may
be seen as the partial embodiment of ideal excellence. On the whole,
moral agents can be paradigms for specific virtues without being para-

digms of supreme ideals. In this way, PIs can function as standards of inspiration and at the same time furnish us exemplars for the intrinsic actuation of moral ideals. They are thus the concrete foci of ideal achievement and not mere models for imitation. In the manner in which they have a transforming significance in the life of certain moral agents, they furnish us a basic guide to the understanding of moral creativity.

The foregoing remarks assume the prospective point of view. This is not to deny that PIs can also function retrospectively as standards of judgment of conduct. Moral agents can appeal to their PIs for determination of moral judgments instead of directly appealing to the embodied ideals and rules in the moral practice. This at any rate seems to be true to Confucian moral agents, as we shall see in the following chapters on Confucian ethics.

By way of conclusion we may note the following points that emerge from our exploration of the role of PIs in moral practices:

1. The PIs give an actuating significance to a moral practice or cultural way of life. They furnish us exemplars of intrinsic actuation of moral rules and ideals implicit in their moral practices.

2. By their insight into the human condition, they infuse vitality to moral ideals by embodying them in their lives and conduct.

3. By their styles of orientation to their own moral traditions, they may become themselves points of moral orientation or beacons of light, thus functioning as standards of inspiration for commitive moral agents.

Creative moral agency is perhaps best understood in terms of the role and function of PIs. It is hoped that a further exploration of the notion of PI in a particular moral practice can throw light also upon its significance to moral theory.

4

An Excursion to Confucian Ethics

We now turn to a normative ethics which underlies Confucian morality. Our primary interest lies in a further elucidation of the significance of the notion of paradigmatic individuals in relation to an actual moral practice. Confucian ethics is chosen for this purpose because of its distinctive and peculiar emphasis on the role of paradigmatic individuals in both moral teaching and performance. Confucian ethics, apart from its intrinsic importance to the understanding of Chinese thought, furnishes an example of an ethics which forms an interesting contrast to the ethics of rules and principles dominant in modern philosophical literature. Our excursion also in part reflects my own attempt to understand my moral background.

Although our main interest lies in the explication of the Confucian notion of paradigmatic individuals, the task cannot be adequately carried out without a prior understanding of the context in which this notion functions. This necessitates a discussion of the structure of Confucian ethics which forms the central aim of the present chapter.

The term "Confucian ethics," or "the ethics of Confucius," is used here to designate the principal features of the ethical doctrine found in the *Analects* of Confucius. Any attempt to expound the structure of Confucian ethics is initially beset by a major problem, for Confucian ethics does not appear to admit of a systematic treatment. The preceptorial sayings of Confucius, which formed a principal and authoritative source of Chinese moral education until 1949, do not appear in a logical and coherent order. The concrete and performative significance of precepts, advice, injunctions, and examples is not expounded in terms of either rules of relevance or rules of inference. There is, most conspicuously, an absence of definitions of essential concepts that purport to guide the various topics of conversation, which may well be considered a mark of merit.[1] For in the teachings of Confucius, there is "an absence of dogma, a clear realization of the necessity of suspended judgment, and an espousal of intellectual democracy."[2] This noteworthy quality may also be viewed as characteristic of the Chinese attitude toward ethical theory. Arthur Hummel, writing in 1952, observed that in China "the subject matter of ethics or discussion of ethical problems seldom degenerated into cant or hackneyed topic of conversation. It was everybody's business. It concerned living issues and actual situations, and therefore could not easily be smothered in dogma, or evaporate in platitudes or philosophical theory."[3]

The unsystematic character of the ethics of Confucius, however, is dominated by a certain focal unity. Quite obviously, Confucian ethics in the *Analects* cannot be treated as a moral theory in the sense that it explicitly sets forth a theory of moral judgments or an analysis of moral concepts in their systemic relation and application. But if such an ethics is to be considered relevant to contemporary moral theory and practice, there is a need to present the doctrine in a language amenable to critical appraisal.[4] The present chapter therefore aims at a discussion of certain features of Confucian ethics in the idiom of contemporary moral philosophy. In this discussion an attempt is made to articulate a structure of Confucian ethics that relates its central concepts of *jên*, *li*, and *chün-tzu*.[5] The notion of *chün-tzu*, which expresses a conception of paradigmatic individuals, will receive further attention in the following chapter.

A. *Jên as an Internal Criterion of Morality*

Confucius remarked that he seeks "a unity all pervading" (*Analects*, XV.2).[6] In view of the frequent occurrence of the word "*jên*" and certain remarks that suggest a "central thread" (IV.15, XV.23), an exponent of Confucian ethics is quite justified in construing the different occurrences of "*jên*" as pointing to a thematic unity.[7] The various uses of "*jên*" may be considered as so many devices that draw our attention to, and focus on the concrete relevance of, the central importance of an ideal way of life. This unity of normative focus does not preclude the concept from being a term of plurisignation, a term that possesses, as it were, a power to suggest and stimulate different thoughts and interpretations.[8] Thus the concept has been rendered as "perfect virtue," "goodness," "humanity," "human-heartedness," "manhood-at-its-best," "love," "compassion"—terms that are by no means equivalent in meaning. There can be little doubt that all these renderings are attempts at capturing the central normative focus of Confucian ethics. In the *Analects* there are many remarks about *jên*, but they are not all of the same logical import or order of generality. Here we regard these remarks not as an implicit attempt at a definition of the concept but as an articulation and specification in the context of a moral ideal of Confucius. An interesting question arises: Can one introduce, in other words, *a way of speaking* that effectively unveils the structure of insights in the uses of *"jên"*? In dealing with this question we must pay heed to two sorts of uses of *"jên"* among the remarks in the *Analects*.

In his insightful study of the concept *jên,* Chan points out that the concept is subject to a particular and general interpretation. As referring to a particular virtue, *jên* occasionally occurred in pre-Confucian texts meaning the "kindness of a ruler to his people" (p. 296). Chan states that

> instead of perpetrating the ancient understanding of *jên* as a particular virtue, he [Confucius] transformed it into what Legge very appropriately translated as perfect virtue and Waley as Goodness. To be sure, in a few cases *jên* is still used by Confucius as a particular virtue. For example, in *Analects* IV.2; VI.21; IX.28 (repeated in XIV.30); XV.32; and XVII.8, *jên* is contrasted with knowledge, wisdom, courage, or propriety. In this narrow sense, *jên* is best translated as "benevolence" as Legge has done. In all other cases, however, *jên* connotes the general meaning of moral life at its best. (p. 297)

Being a thematic unity of Confucian discourses, *jên* in its general meaning of "moral life at its best" or alternatively "moral excellence" is the central preoccupation of Confucian ethics. However, the distinction between *jên* in its general meaning as moral excellence (henceforth Jg) and *jên* as a particular virtue (henceforth Jp) raises an important question concerning their relation. A discussion of the relation between Jg and Jp will throw light on the general relation between Jg and other particular virtues, and also on an aspect of the nature and function of Jg.

With respect to Jp two not necessarily incompatible views are possible. First, we may regard Jp simply as an exemplification of Jg in the sense that any piece of conduct to be called *"jên"* must satisfy the requirements of Jg. Jg here would function as a general principle of moral judgments whether of action or character of persons. Jg would be a principle of justification, which Hu Shih termed "the general principle of conduct" (Chan, p. 298). It is Jg that determines the nature of moral judgments and actions. Second, we can also view Jp as a realization *in concreto* of a particular moral disposition. There are, of course, other equally important moral dispositions. In this view, Jp as a particular piece of moral conduct has the same value status as the actualizations of other morally commendable dispositions, e.g., wisdom, courage, righteousness, sincerity, loyalty, filial piety, and other virtues mentioned in the *Analects*.

The distinction between the two views may be clarified as follows. The first view regards Jg as a device for casting particular actions into a predetermined mode. Jg here functions as a *retrospective* standard for moral judgments. Any action, from this retrospective viewpoint, has a determinate character prescribed by Jg. As we shall later observe, Jg may be explicated in terms of a Confucian Golden Rule (*chung* and *shu*). Thus actions as subject to judgment have a determinate character in accordance with a rule of Jg. The question "What shall I do?" is on this view a determination of an action as having the definite character of a past deed. In this sense, Jp would simply be an instance of Jg. In the second view, Jp is a *particularization* of Jg. Jg is an ideal to be realized. It is Jp as a realization of Jg that gives Jg a determinate character. Jg may be said to have a *prospective* function that acquires content in the actions that are said to be its realizations. If we are not mistaken, it is Jg in its prospective function that forms the central emphasis in Confucian ethics.[9] The emphasis is on the importance of personal cultivation in the realization of *jên*, but this does not preclude Jg from functioning also as a principle of moral judgments. In the prospective view of Jg the moral agent seeks to bring into existence an ideal state of affairs. The accent here is on *doing* rather than on *judging*. From the retrospective view of Jg, Jp and all particular virtues are forms of moral excellence. Jg is a supreme principle of justification in the sense that all moral assessment is subject to a standard determination of Jg.

What then is the nature of Jg or the ideal of moral excellence which Confucius urged his disciples to realize? As an ideal, it would be a possible state of affairs that is excellent or intrinsically valuable to which the moral aspirants must be prepared to sacrifice themselves. We are told that "the determined scholar and the man of virtue (*jên*) will not seek to live at the expense of injuring their virtue." They will even go to the extent of sacrificing "their lives to preserve their virtue complete" (XV.8). Or again, "the man, who in the view of gain, thinks of righteousness (*i*); who in the view of danger is prepared to give up his life; and who does not forget an old agreement however far back it extends: —such a man may be reckoned a complete man" (XIV.13). Chan is inclined to the view of Jg as an *inclusive* virtue. This is supported by certain remarks in the *Analects*. According to Chan, *jên* "includes filial piety (XVII.21), wisdom (V.18), propriety (XII.1), courage (XIV.5), and loyalty to government (V.18; XVIII.1); it requires the practice of earnestness, liberality, truthfulness, diligence, and generosity (XVII.6)."[10] In brief, *"jên* precludes all evil and underlies as well as embraces all possible virtues, so much so that if you set your mind on *jên,* you will be free from evil (IV.4)" (p. 298).

The notion of *jên* as an inclusive virtue or end should be distinguished from the notion of paramount end, for the doctrine of inclusive end is "inclusive in the sense that there is no desire or interest which cannot be regarded as a candidate, however unpromising, for a place in the pattern of life."[11] *Jên* cannot be a paramount end in the sense that it is the single dominating aim of the agent's moral activiity to which all other ends or desires are subordinated, since Confucius did not appear to intend in his teachings any hierarchy of ends. Hardie, in a different context, correctly maintains that "the morality of altruism and self-sacrifice is consistent with the doctrine of the inclusive end but not with the more determinate doctrine of the paramount end." Altruism *(shu),* as we shall see, is a rule of *jên.* In its concrete significance, Confucian morality is a morality of self-sacrifice and altruism.

If *jên* is an inclusive virtue, then the possession of particular virtues by the agents would be considered as laudable personal merits, since *jên* includes the presence of these particular virtues.[12] In the abstract, we may speak of *jên* as a unitary principle of particular virtues. On the other hand, if *jên* is in fact realized, it would be a quality of a life of moral excellence—a pervasive or supervenient quality, superadded, so to speak, to the presence of particular virtues. In this sense, *jên* does not literally include particular virtues, but is a sort of "resultant attribute"—a quality that results from the possession of particular virtues. *Jên* in this sense cannot be aimed at directly, particularly in view of the fact that Confucius did not give us a comprehensive description of *jên* as an *ideal* end which all men should seek. I should like to suggest that the articulation of this ideal in effect consists in the characterization of the man who possesses these particular virtues pervaded by *jên* quality. *Jên* is thus the apex of moral achievement. Aside from possessing the particular virtues previously mentioned, a man of *jên,* for example, pays heed to filial and fraternal piety (I.2). Being free from wickedness (IV.4), he can endure both in conditions of adversity and in enjoyments (IV.2). He can truly be said to know how to love or to hate men (IV.3). Wishing to be established himself, "he seeks also to establish others; wishing to be enlarged (or prominent) himself, he seeks also to enlarge others" (VI.28). He judges others by what is *near* in himself (VI.28). He is a master of himself and performs his actions in accordance with *li* or propriety (XII.1). He is, as it were, a measure of good and evil. Here we may note a striking resemblance of this notion of *jên* man to the following passage in the *Nicomachean Ethics* on the happy man.

> The happy man will have the attribute of permanence . . . and he will remain happy throughout his life. For he will always or to the highest degree both do and contemplate what is in conformity with virtue; he will bear the vicissitudes of fortune most nobly and with perfect decorum under all circumstances, inasmuch as he is truly good and "four-square beyond reproach" (I. 1100b).

Jên is, of course, a practical rather than a formal principle of morality. As a practical principle it is a substantive principle for guiding conduct. In answer to the question of Fan Ch'ih about *jên*, Confucius replied that "it is to love all men" (XII.22). It is, I think, an affectionate concern for the welfare of others. The practical and psychological foundation of *jên* rests in filial and fraternal piety (I.2). Here we are confronted with the well-known Confucian doctrine of the gradation of love which Mo-tzu subsequently criticized. The question lies in the interpretation and evaluation of the notion of *degree of love.* If we regard the notion of degree of love as simply that of an emphasis on the immediately possible contexts of action, the Confucian doctrine appears to be plausible. There is, of course, no logical impossibility of our being directly concerned with the welfare of humanity. The question is how we can bring this into a successful fruition in practical conduct. In real life, the boundaries of our actions are, to the Confucian, fairly well-defined by our familial relationships and cultural milieu. The realization of our affectionate concern for humanity is a matter of extending these familial and familiar contexts of action, of enlarging both the range of moral situations and the range of persons. Confronted with moral problems in real life, we cannot embrace the whole of humanity in one view. Our view of the problem is restricted in live contexts. We need not presuppose, as the classical Confucians often do, that the contexts are fairly stable. But the Confucian insight remains that the realization of an ideal of moral excellence is a matter of the extensive possibility of our concern. The substantive nature of *jên,* in effect, is an active and extensive concern for humanity. And if this notion is to be construed as extensive benevolence, then the substantive *jên* principle would be an ideal of extensive benevolence styled with an affectionate regard for others rather than by self-interest.

For a clearer elucidation of this Confucian notion of extensive benevolence, one should distinguish it from the Benthamite utilitarian ideal where the stress is on the consequence, rather than the affectionate regard for others that is independent of consequences of action. An instructive comparison may be made with the views of Francis Hutcheson and Joseph Butler. Hutcheson, for example, compared the "universal benevolence toward all men" with the principle of gravitation, which "*increases* as the distance is diminished, and is *strongest* when Bodys come to touch each other."[13] Butler, in commenting upon the Christian precept of "Love thy neighbor as thyself," remarked that it is concerned with "that part of the universe, that part of mankind, that part of our country, which comes under our immediate notice, acquaintance and influence, and with which we have to do."[14] Whereas Hutcheson seems to put his emphasis on the empirical possibilities of extensive benevolence, Butler draws our attention to the practical and psychological condition of moral agency. This point of view finds a recent echo:

> We must recognize that our capacity for love is limited by the limitations of our knowledge. Love, in the full sense, is only possible for those with whom we are personally acquainted. . . . The personal ideal for each man may be represented by the notion of a focus on those we know personally, extending, in this gradually modified form, to the margin of the whole of humanity.[15]

To the individual as a moral agent, a question still remains: Is there any *rule* that can guide me in extending my concern for others? Is there an internal criterion of morality that will guide me in the realization of the ideal of love? The famous Golden Rule of Confucius may be viewed in light of this question. Confucius' disciple T'san said that "the doctrine of our master is to be true to the principles of our nature (*chung*) and the benevolent exercise of them to others (*shu*)" (IV.15). Again, Tzu-kung asked, "Is there one word which can serve as a rule of practice for all one's life?" To this Confucius replied, "Is not *shu* such a word? What you do not want done to yourself, do not do to others" (XV.23). *Chung* and *shu* as a rule for the practice of *jên* is a rule of reciprocal regard of man to man. *Chung* and *shu* may also be regarded as an internal criterion of morality, in the sense that they are the criterion for determining the appropriate relevance of moral feelings and attitudes. Since the practice of *jên* consists in *chung* and *shu*, *jên* may be said to be an internal criterion of morality. *Chung* refers to the sincerity of our commitment to moral principles as principles of action; *shu* indicates the other-regarding nature of these principles. Thus an agent, in his own effort at moral cultivation, aims also at the cultivation of other agents. This is the method of the man of *jên* referred to earlier.

To summarize our discussion of *jên* in this section, we may state that *jên*, as an ideal of moral excellence—the central thread of Confucian ethics—is an ideal of an inclusive virtue. As a substantive principle of conduct, it is the "love of all men" in the sense of an affectionate concern for the welfare of others. The method for the realization of *jên* in practice is extensive benevolence, governed by the Golden Rule. Since the Golden Rule (*chung* and *shu*) functions as an internal criterion for the determination of personal moral conduct, *jên* may be said to be an *internal* criterion of Confucian morality, for its emphasis is on the personal aspect of moral agency. We still need to inquire into the interpersonal setting of moral action (the Confucian notion of *li* or propriety) and its relation to *jên*.

B. Li as an External Criterion of Morality[16]

It is quite plausibly an implicit view of Confucius that man is a being of feelings, impulses, and desires. The morality of *jên* is in effect intended as a way to endow these feelings, impulses, and desires with a significance beyond their *de facto* character. As betokened by the Golden Rule of *chung* and *shu*, *jên* is an internal criterion for the cultivation of appropriate *human* attitudes toward these feelings. The emphasis here seems to be on self-cultivation or the establishment of moral character in the realization of the ideal of moral excellence, substantively expressed in the love of humanity. This emphasis appears to be deficient without a corresponding emphasis on the importance of a criterion for the outward expression of the moral agent's interior life. I suggest that we regard the Confucian concept of *li*, or propriety, as an external criterion of the morality of *jên* in the sense that it is a criterion that governs the concrete expression of *jên*.

Again, we may note that the Confucian concept of *li* is subject to both a particular and a general interpretation. *Li* may be regarded as a set of ritual rules or manners of civility that govern human behavior in different contexts of life situations. In this particular sense, *li* is subject to codification. As one may gather from a reading of the book *Li Chi*, rituals can be very specific and detailed in the regulation of behavior in different situations. Regarding the other sense of *li*, Waley calls our attention to the fact that "it was with the relation of ritual as a whole to morality and not with the details of etiquette and precedence that the early Confucians were chiefly concerned."[17] It is the general sense of *li* that is the central preoccupation of Confucian ethics. Confucius loved the rituals (III.17), but he asked, "If a man be without *jên*, what has he to do with *li*?" (III.3). Moreover, *jên* is said to be in practice constituted by the subduing of oneself (self-mastery) and returning to *li*, and "if a man can for one day subdue himself and return to *li*, all under heaven will ascribe perfect virtue to him" (XII.1). The concept of *li* is thus in its general sense intimately related to the concept of *jên*. The one cannot do without the other.

The general sense of *li* is the moral significance that underlies behavior in conformity to the rules of propriety or ritual rules. According to Confucius' disciple Yu-tzu, one of the most valuable functions of *li* is the establishment of harmony (I.3). We are also told that *li* is indispensable in the cultivation of moral character (VIII.8; XVI.13; XX.3). As a matter of fact, some human dispositions cannot be regarded as personal merits without *li:* "respectfulness, without the rules of propriety, becomes laborious bustle; carefulness, without the rules of propriety, becomes timidity; boldness, without the rules of propriety, becomes insubordination; straightforwardness, without the rules of propriety, becomes rudeness" (VIII.2). In particular, the practice of filial piety, which is a "root" of *jên*, must accord with the rules of propriety (II.5). In conforming to the rules of propriety, reverence (II.7) rather than minute observances (III.4) is essential. If *li* is the outward expression of inner feelings, *jên* is the inward and moral dimension of *li* performances.

Confucius cherished rituals, but he realized the requirements for the complex and minute details of ornamentation and of bodily movements and gestures could be inadvertently misinterpreted. It is also easy for one to fail in ritual performance. But it is the significant *intention* that underlies rituals which forms the normative force of a ritual performance. Moreover, the rituals not only can be observed mechanically as a matter of habit but also may be performed insincerely. In this emphasis on *li* as an important requirement for virtuous actions, it is perhaps the implicit intention of Confucius to suggest the necessity of an outward criterion for successful moral performances. The Confucian view may be stated thus: without *li* or rules of propriety human actions would degenerate into mere movements—mere occurrences without normative significance. The normative significance of ritual actions ultimately lies in *jên*. But mere *jên* feelings and dispositions are by themselves incapable of concrete fulfillment when they are expressed in inappropriate contexts. Thus if *jên* is to be properly regarded as an internal criterion for the moral relevance of feelings, *li* expresses the outward or external criterion for the relevance of the *expressions* of these feelings.

It can be seen that although Confucian ethics does not provide a set of rules of inference from which practical actions can be logically deduced, it does suggest two different kinds of criteria for the identification of the morality of feelings and their appropriate expression. The practical import of these criteria lies in this: a moral agent must aim not only at the cultivation of *right* feelings, but also at the right expression of these feelings in the proper context. There are then two aspects of a moral action: inward rightness and outward rightness. To do what is right in context, one must not only have the right feelings but also express those feelings *rightly*. This is perhaps the *peculiar* feature of the Confucian notion of moral action. A moral action, on this view, can be *completely* described only in terms of the satisfaction of both the internal *jên* criterion and external *li* criterion. What is thus a single description of moral action is, to the Western eye, a duality of logically independent descriptions: a description of an action as conforming to a moral standard or rule, and a description of the *style* or manner of performance. In other words, the Confucian notion of moral action is one in which *jên* feeling is expressed and fulfilled in action in accordance with *li*. A full description would thus involve not merely citing the appropriate feelings and attitudes but also executing them in accordance with ritual rules.

Since these ritual rules are an embodiment of tradition, we may regard *li* as defining the conventionally accepted *style* of action, i.e., the form and possibility of moral achievement within the cultural setting or cultural life style. *Li,* unlike *jên,* does not define the nature of morality, but only the limiting form of execution of moral performance. In a more contemporary idiom, we may express this idea in terms of the *tie* or *contact* of an individual agent's actions with the cultural way of life which gives them the locus of identification and the possibility of moral achievement. An appropriate action, as conforming to the ritual requirements of *li,* may be identified as a moral action insofar as it is pervaded by a concern for *jên.* If one wants to lay more stress on the importance of *li,* then one may say that particular moral actions are partial exemplifications of a cultural life style. A Confucian agent's respect for *li* or cultural life style is at the same time a respect for the reality of the situation, the background and possibility that furnish the contexts for successful moral performance. This emphasis on *li* is one possible justification for the Confucian homage to the concrete. Every action, on this view, has a *conventional* aspect for understanding its normative meaning and import. Whether or not we accept this stress on *li,* some sort of convention for identifying the normative import of action must be an essential element in any moral theory that aims at an assessment of actions in terms of right and wrong.

If the humanity of man lies in *jên,* and *jên* cannot be without *li, li* may be regarded as a humanizing instrument for the moral education of man. Fingarette sees the significance of *li* in this light. "Men become truly human as their raw impulse is shaped by *li.* And *li* is the fulfillment of human impulse, the civilized expression of it—not a formalistic dehumanization. *Li* is the specifically humanizing form of the dynamic relation of man-to-man."[18] From the point of view of *jên* morality, *li* is a humanizing agency precisely because rituals define the restraining orbit of the expression of *jên.* As Hsün-tzu later clearly saw, *li* is the road to *jên* and *i* (righteousness). The ritual rules "present us with models, but no explanations." They are the "markers" of the Way of *Jên,* not its substance.[19] As *markers* of the Way of *Jên,* they are tied to the individual's duties and stations in life; for it is in playing these social roles that one can hope to achieve in the concrete his moral ideal of excellence. Traditional conventions and mores encapsulated in ritual rules thus provide the limiting forms of moral action. Negligence of these limiting forms can lead to a failure in moral achievement. We previously observed that for a Confucian, a moral action must satisfy both the internal and external criteria, for these define both the moral significance of feelings and the appropriate setting for the expression of these feelings. *Li* as ritualistic propriety cannot be reduced to mere formality. For a failure in conforming to the requirement of a particular rule of propriety is a *formal* error, but a failure in embodying *jên* in ritual conduct is a material error. The success of the one depends on the agent's knowledge of the ritual rules, the other on the agent's own moral character. It is, as we shall later observe, in the ideal of *chün-tzu* or the superior man that embodies the union of *jên* and *li.*

The emphasis on *jên* alone or the internal criterion of morality may lead to a characterization of Confucian ethics as an *ethics of character.* From the point of view of the importance of moral education, this emphasis is quite justified. Confucius would have agreed with Aristotle that moral virtues are habits in the sense of cultivation of appropriate dispositions for the conduct of life. On the other hand, mere emphasis on the external criterion, or *li,* may lead to a characterization of Confucian ethics as an *ethics of ritual rules* or ritual formalism. The justification perhaps partially lies in this: even if a person is properly cultivated, the concrete expression of his moral attitudes and feelings must be deemed relevant and appropriate to the circumstances in society. In other words, Confucian ethics sees the need for accepted procedures for the expression of moral feelings and attitudes.

In stressing the interdependence of *jên* and *li,* Confucian ethics may be properly called an "ethics of role," since *li* embodies the rituals for the performance of social roles. As an ethics of role, Confucian ethics can be of significant interest to moral philosophy. As examples of recent attention to the concept of role for ethics, one may think of the works of Dorothy Emmet and Bernard Mayo.[20] In a recent essay, Mayo maintains that "in the history of thinking about moral concepts, there are two poles [the ethics of character and the ethics of rule]." These "are respectively symbolized or exemplified by: the right act, and the good man (and their contraries); the lawgiver, and the paragon." Mayo himself is inclined to the view that

> rather than being distinct but intimately and puzzlingly related, as are the other two, role-morality is not distinct, though it offers a useful new approach to the other two. It is not distinct, because the demands of one's role can be represented either as more or less formalized rules—this will be the case, for instance, with professional "ethics"—or as the requirement of certain postures, attitudes or qualities of conduct, as in the case of Sartre's waiter (or even Kant's grocer), family relationships, or the military ethos.[21]

Whether or not the ethics of character is to be viewed as distinct from the ethics of rule, Confucian ethics as an ethics of role does suggest their interdependence and intimate relationship. To insist on the necessity of *jên* in ritual conduct is to urge that we adopt a moral attitude toward social roles. From this moral point of view not all social roles have the same normative weight. On the other hand, to emphasize the necessity of *li* in the expression of moral feelings and attitudes is to acknowledge the fact that it is in the *li* as embodying the rituals for the performance of social roles that a moral agent can hope to bring the morality of *jên* into a successful fruition. In other words, it is in the social context of *li* that the morality of *jên* attains its practical effectuation.[22]

Even apart from its connection with *jên* and social roles, one may also note the significance of the use of proper language in the performance of rituals. Fingarette, in the spirit of the works of J.L. Austin on performative utterances, states:

> It is . . . in the medium of ceremony that the peculiarly human part of our life is lived. The ceremonial act is the primary, irreducible event; language cannot be understood in isolation from the conventional practice in which it is rooted; conventional practice cannot be understood in isolation from the language which defines and is part of it. No purely physical motion is a promise; no word alone, independent of the ceremonial contexts, circumstances, and roles can be a promise. Word and motion are only abstractions from concrete ceremonial act.[23]

Fingarette thinks that "the text of the *Analects,* in letter and spirit, supports and enriches our own quite recently emerging vision of man as a ceremonial being."[24] A Confucian would certainly appreciate this credit to an important insight of man as a *ceremonial* being, but he would perhaps add, quite in consonance with the spirit of Confucius' teachings, that man is a *historical* being, for the personal history of a moral agent is also tied to his cultural history. As a ceremonial being, man is a species of the historical, for *li* in its embodiment of ritual formulas for action is in actuality an embodiment of historic tradition, a cultural way of life. Confucius thought of himself as "a transmitter and not a maker, believing in and loving the ancients" (VII.1); as a man not born "in the possession of knowledge" but one "who is fond of antiquity, and earnest in seeking it there" (VII.19). This modesty of claim to wisdom in effect conceals his view of the historical tradition as embodied in *li.* One need not here endorse his reverential attitude toward history, but in his emphasis on the importance of tradition in moral conduct, one is drawn to the fact that man is irrevocably a historical being. His historicity lies in the continuity of his moral conduct to his moral practice. Moral language, if it is to be regarded as ceremonially performative, thus embodies a tradition. Interpreting language in the normative sense, a Confucian would perhaps concur with Whitehead's observation: "Each language embalms an historic tradition. Each language is the civilization of expression in the social systems which use it. Language is the systematization of expression."[25] The use of ritual language may be said to be symbolic of the "happening" of a tradition. In ritual performance, an individual agent integrates his action with his cultural history. To a Confucian, a ritual act is, as it were, a way of putting one's signature on a provided form. It is a performance signifying endorsement of a tradition, an expression of a cultural style of life. To Confucius the signature must bear the stamp of the morality of *jên*. Just as *jên* cannot be without *li, li* would degenerate into an artificial, though perhaps aesthetic, form—a mere ostentation or ornamentation—without the morality of *jên*.

C. Chün-tzu as an Ideal of a Paradigmatic Individual

Confucius, being a lover of antiquity, claimed to be merely a transmitter rather than an originator of wisdom. This modesty, aside from expressing his reverential attitude toward antiquity, conceals his earnest quest for men who would satisfy his vision of a morally perfect man—the man of *jên* who achieves throughout his life the ideal of moral excellence. Even his own paragons of virtue Yao and Shun (VIII.18; VII.19)—his historical paradigms—fell short of his vision. His remarks on *chün-tzu*, or the superior man, seem to represent an attempt to articulate the practically realizable ideal of a morally good man, not as a perfect man free from errors, but as a man of moral distinction who can serve as a guideline for the ultimate realization of the morality of *jên*. *Chün-tzu* is the idea of a man in whom *jên* and *li* are embodied in personal harmony; it is the personal embodiment of both the internal and external criteria of morality. He is, in the words of Confucius, one in whom "substance and refinement are properly blended" (VI.16).

The next chapter presents a more detailed discussion of the notion of *chün-tzu* as a paradigmatic individual who serves a standard-guiding function for Confucian moral agents. Here we simply take note of the notion of *chün-tzu* as an idea of a man of moral distinction who cherishes *jên* and *li* in actual conduct. The significance of *chün-tzu* as a paradigmatic individual perhaps lies in this: the practical morality of *jên* cannot be merely a matter of theoretical instruction, for moral action is a union of internal and external criteria in the concrete situations of the life of moral agents. To look to a *chün-tzu* for guidance is to find an actuating force in one's commitment to *jên* morality. Mere instruction and advice are not as effective in moving men to the practice of *jên* and *li*. The insight of Confucius thus lies in the vision of a superior man as a paradigmatic standard of conduct. Confucius himself, for most Chinese in their long and continuing history until recent decades, has been regarded as a paradigmatic individual, a man of moral distinction who serves both as a standard of inspiration and as a standard of aspiration for Confucian moral agents.

The Confucian notion of *chün-tzu* may thus be regarded as an articulation of a normative paradigmatic individual. *Chün-tzu* embodies *jên* in ritual conduct. For Confucius, the necessity of introducing the conception of *chün-tzu* perhaps lies in this: though he enunciates a Golden Rule, which purports to govern human relations, and insists on the necessity of the ritual rules, there are still no specific precepts to guide the actions of the moral agent in particular situations. *Chün-tzu* provides not only a moving force to the realization of *jên,* but also certain precepts that directly bear on practical situations. An appeal to the notion of *chün-tzu* is in effect an appeal to what a good man would do under such-and-such circumstance. I can recall in my youth, among classmates in a Chinese high school, the frequency with which they appealed to the notion of *chün-tzu,* as contrasted with *hsiao-jên* (inferior man), to express their moral disapproval of some particular conduct. Perhaps, for most men with a Confucian upbringing, *chün-tzu* has this practical function. *Chün-tzu* serves not merely this retrospective function for the judgment of conduct, but also a prospective function. In appealing to the notion of *chün-tzu* in its retrospective function, the Confucian moral agent asks: How would a *chün-tzu judge* this or that piece of conduct? In its prospective function, the question is: What would a *chün-tzu do* in such a situation?[26]

The notion of *chün-tzu* can be said to make concrete the linking up of *jên* and *li*, the elan, zest, and spirit with which a moral act is performed. In Confucian ethics, the notion of *chün-tzu* may be said to be an *actuating* principle of *jên* and *li* in that it provides an active agency for the realization of *jên* morality within the orbit of ritual performance. Here it is not a question of providing sanction as a motivating reason for morality of action, but of providing an inspiring force to *jên* in the life of the moral agents, thus endowing, so to speak, the union of *jên* and *li* with dynamic properties in conduct. In the abstract, all the three notions of *jên, li,* and *chün-tzu* are separate principles of action; but in the concrete, all three are dimensions of moral focus that dominate respectively in the various and varying contexts of actions. To be a *chün-tzu* is to inspire *jên* and *li* with an active character. There can be degrees of moral achievement in the personal history of different moral agents.

In this chapter, I have attempted a reconstruction of Confucian ethics in terms of a relation of three principal concepts found in the *Analects*. We have discussed these in the idiom familiar to students of moral philosophy. Confucian ethics may be regarded as an ethics of role since *jên* as an internal criterion and *li* as an external criterion of morality find their interdependence in role performance. The notion of *chün-tzu* as a paradigmatic individual may be seen as an attempt to give a *moving* force to the ethical doctrine of *jên* and *li*, for it is in *chün-tzu* that one finds a paradigmatic individual's embodiment of *jên* and *li*. I hope that the insights of Confucius thus may be seen in contemporary terms. The present chapter may be viewed as an attempt at a preliminary assessment of Confucian ethics. If the account given is judged to be of some plausibility and of philosophical interest, Confucian ethics, in the manner in which it permits the discussion and reflection of important ethical questions, may be seen as a significant contribution to the literature of moral philosophy.

5

Confucian Paradigmatic Individuals

In this chapter we focus on one basic feature of Confucian ethics as an ethics of flexibility to further examine Confucius' conception of paradigmatic individuals (*chün-tzu*). We begin by again characterizing *chün-tzu* as having a standard-guiding function for Confucian agents. Section 5A offers an attempt at a critical reconstruction and assessment of the notion of *chün-tzu*. Section 5B takes up a feature of our account in terms of the problem of rules and exceptions, which is best dealt with by making a distinction between normal and exigent situations—a distinction that appears to be implicit in the Confucian doctrine of *ching ch'uan*. Viewed in this light, the flexible character of Confucian ethics can be seen to have an important bearing on a problem in moral philosophy.

A. Chün-tzu: A Further Characterization

We now turn to our immediate task, a more detailed discussion of Confucian paradigmatic individuals or *chün-tzu*. Our interest here is to reconstruct this Confucian notion and inquire into the plausibility and significance of this notion as an underlying theme of Confucian ethics. I believe that in the notion of *chün-tzu* we find a fairly persuasive exemplification of the three summary features of PI discussed in Chapter 3: as giving an actuating significance to a moral practice; as expressing insight into human conditions or the reality of the human situation; and as expressing styles of orientation to a moral practice that serve a standard-guiding function. The notion of *chün-tzu* is a notion of creative agency within a moral practice, for as we shall see, a *chün-tzu* combines respect for moral practice and adaptability in the face of changing circumstances of human life. Confucian ethics, as it has been noted by some scholars and sinologists, is an ethics of flexibility. In the words of a recent historian, "The chief strength of Confucianism is its flexibility, a remarkable quality that enables it to resist all pressures and to face all adversities."[1]

Although Confucius believed that only a sage (*sheng jen*), divinely inspired and innately wise, could envision and establish a harmonious social order, the ideal of sagehood was not regarded by him as practically attainable by ordinary moral agents. He once remarked that he could not ever hope to meet a *sheng jen,* but only a *chün-tzu* (VII.25).[2] The ideal sagehood, in his mind, functions more like a supreme but abstract ideal of a perfect moral personality, an imagined vision rather than a possible objective of the moral life. Thus he more often discoursed on the conduct and quality of *chün-tzu* than on the nature of sagehood. In general, the notion of *chün-tzu* is a notion of a man of moral excellence, of a paradigmatic individual who sets the tone and quality of the life of ordinary moral agents. As previously noted, a *chün-tzu* is a man who embodies *jên* and *li.* As a guiding paradigm, every man can strive to become *chün-tzu* rather than *hsiao-jên* (inferior man). There are of course degrees of personal achievement depending on the situation, character, ability, and opportunity of moral agents. The translation of "*chün-tzu*" as "superior man" forcefully brings out the *chün-tzu*'s superiority of moral character and aptitude.[3] The translation of *chün-tzu* as "true gentleman" focuses on the *chün-tzu*'s relation with the cultural setting of his actions, his ability to satisfy, so to speak, the stylistic requirements of a moral practice.[4] A *chün-tzu,* in this sense, is an embodiment of a cultural life style.

The varying remarks on *chün-tzu* in the *Analects* may be regarded as setting forth the different requirements or qualities for a life of moral excellence. A *chün-tzu,* embodying *jên* and *li,* is also a man of righteousness (*i*), of catholicity and neutrality, in whom words and deeds are in harmony. The discussion that follows relates to these prominent features in the notion of *chün-tzu.*

A man of righteousness (i). Confucius remarked that "the superior man, extensively studying all learning and keeping himself under the restraint of the rules of propriety (*li*), may thus likewise not overstep [the boundary of] what is right (*i*)" (VI.25). The *chün-tzu* is said to hold righteousness (*i*) to be of the highest importance (XVII .23).[5] *I* is contrasted with profit to bring out the Confucian distinction between morality and egoism (IV.16). The notion of *i,* not elucidated in the *Analects,* is a difficult notion. It may be variously rendered as "righteousness," "right conduct," "moral principle or standard," or "the doing of what is right." All these renderings perhaps suggest different aspects of *i*. Insofar as *i* is opposed to profit, *i* may be taken as characterizing the Confucian Moral Point of View. *I*, like courage, knowledge, etc., would also seem to be a particular virtue (i.e., righteousness) that results from the correctness of moral performance. If *li* defines an aspect of right act in *jên* morality, it is an emphasis on the *tie* between actions and the cultural life style. *I*, on the other hand, gives us a sense of rightness as relating to the concrete problematic situation that calls for moral action inspired by *jên*. According to Fung, "Righteousness (*i*) means the 'oughtness' of a situation. *I* is a categorical imperative. Every one in society has certain things which he ought to do, and which must be done for their sake, because they are the morally right thing to do."[6] However, the "oughtness" of the situation, though a characteristic of obligatory actions, has its central focus on the right act as appropriate to the particular situation that a moral agent confronts. Doing what is right in a situation is not a mere matter of conformity with moral and ritual rules, but also conformity to a *judgment* of their relevance and vindication in actual situations. *I* is another focus on an aspect of the concrete. If *li* is the emphasis on the contact between *jên* morality and the cultural life style, *i* is on the contact between *jên* morality and actual situations. Thus the judgment of what is to be done is reserved to the moral agent. Confucius remarked, "The superior man in *everything* considers righteousness (*i*) to be essential. He performs it according to the rules of propriety (*li*). He brings it forth in humility. He completes it with sincerity. This is indeed a superior man" (XV.17). This passage brings out the relationship of *li* and *i*. Our exposition of *i*, if it is correct, focuses on a view of the nature of moral action as an action in accordance with a judgment of the relevance of moral rules to concrete situations that occur within the settings of a cultural life style.

We may sum up the significance of the preceding requirements for *chün-tzu*. A *chün-tzu* is a man of *jên, li,* and *i*. The concept of *jên* is the concept of an ideal of moral excellence. It is the *jên* quality that pervades the life of a *chün-tzu*. This is the focal point of his paradigmatic standard-guiding function for ordinary moral agents. *Jên* and other particular virtues portray the inner aspect of Confucian ethics. This focus gives us a pervasive and underlying feature of Confucian morality. The focus is on man himself and what he can morally accomplish in relation to others. This latter emphasis deals with the social and cultural setting of moral performance—the ritual context (*li*) in which human transactions occur with varying import of interests and motives.

Li gives the moral action a locale of normative identification and an orbit of restraining conditions for the proper achievement of the moral ideal. Actions that conform to *li* requirements may be said to be in contact with the cultural life style. If *li* focuses on the *tie* of individual actions to culture, the freedom of a moral agent is radically limited in what he *can* do and accomplish. However, the restraining function of *li* defines only the *form* but not the *content* of this freedom. The emphasis on *i* as a requirement of being a *chün-tzu* preserves a great deal of latitude in action. Just as *jên* cannot be practiced without *li*, or the cultural setting, *jên* cannot be realized without *i*, or judgment of the relevance of *jên* and *li* to concrete situations of moral performance. It is *i* that establishes the contact between actions and the actual situations that confront the moral agent. Our next two sets of descriptions of *chün-tzu*, together with the present account, explain in large part this flexible and adaptable feature of Confucian ethics.

A man of catholicity and neutrality. "The superior man is broadminded and not partisan; the inferior man is partisan but not broadminded" (II.14; also VII.30). The superior man is not like an implement (intended only for a narrow and specific purpose) (II.12). Instead, "he should have broad vision, wide interests, and sufficient ability to do many things."[7] He is a man of moral integrity that exemplifies itself even in the face of great emergency (VIII.8). He aims at "the higher things or principles" (XIV.14), and is dignified without being proud (XIII.26).

The foregoing remarks on the aptitude and broadmindedness of a *chün-tzu* may be anticipated in view of Confucius' emphasis on *jên, li,* and *i.* If *jên* consists in the affectionate concern in varying degrees for humanity, it requires from the moral agent the ability to "know men" and sympathize with the being and predicaments of other moral agents. However, the ability to execute one's moral intentions within ritual contexts is also important. If *i* is required to give an actuating import to *jên* and *li,* then the *chün-tzu* must exercise that "secret art" that gives a practical effectuation to his moral nature as an exemplary guidance to the conduct of other agents. This theme of contagion of the *chün-tzu*'s conduct in Confucius' thinking is perhaps best expressed in *Chung Yung.* "The way which the superior man pursues, reaches wide and far, and yet is secret. . . . The way of the superior man may be found, in its simple elements, in the intercourse of common men and women; but in its utmost reaches, it shines brightly through heaven and earth." "The superior man can find himself in no situation in which he is not himself."[8] Although the *chün-tzu's* way is secret and capable of effusive influence in the lives of ordinary moral agents, he does not remain a mere spectator of human behavior, for he *"seeks to perfect the admirable qualities of men, and does not seek* to perfect their bad qualities" (XII.16). Being a man of *jên*, he wishes to establish his own character and also the character of others. Confucius said, "To be able to judge *of others* by what is nigh *in ourselves;*—this may be called the art of virtue (*jên*)" (VI.28).

This "secret way" or art of the *chün-tzu* is not a mere matter of actions as intellectually determined by moral and ritual rules. If a *chün-tzu* has a natural preference for *jên* morality, this preference does not commit him to specific courses of action prior to a confrontation with an occurrent moral situation. Thus Confucius said of himself, "I have no course for which I am predetermined, and no course against which I am predetermined" (XVIII.8).[9] Moral actions, in concrete contexts, are not a straightforward deduction from given moral rules. The mere intellectual determination of the morality of action does not suffice in the assessment of moral performance, for the relevance of moral and ritual rules must be assessed in concrete situations. This flexible and varying function of *i* accounts for the neutrality of the *chün-tzu's* attitude or lack of commitment to specific courses of action. The actual assessment of moral and ritual rules is at the same time a way of vindicating their actual importance in human life. This act of assessment requires a neutral attitude. It is also this neutral attitude of the *chün-tzu* that gives scope to the exercise of *i* in novel and exigent situations. Thus a *chün-tzu* "in the world, does not set his mind either for anything, or against anything; what is right (*i*) he will follow" (IV.10). He is said to be "satisfied and composed" (VII.36) and free from anxiety, fear, and perplexities (XIV.30; XIL.6). Being a man of *jên*, he is free from anxiety about acting contrary to morality; being a man of courage, he is free from perplexities (XIV.30). His *easeful* life is more a matter of attitude and confidence in his ability to deal with difficult and varying situations than an exemplification of his infallible judgment and authority. This aspect of the notion of *chün-tzu* poses a problem in Confucian ethics. How can a man of virtue (*jên*) and moral integrity be indifferent to specific courses of action that follow from his espoused set of moral principles and rules? If a moral agent is to serve as paradigmatic guidance for actual conduct, it seems reasonable and proper to expect from him specific commitments to what he will do in accordance with moral rules. In Confucian ethics, moral rules and expected types of obligatory actions are by and large a matter of social roles within the cultural lifestyle (*li*). If a *chün-tzu* is a man of *li,* it seems reasonable to expect from him at least a commitment to the application of these moral rules in concrete situations. We shall reserve the exploration of this problem for Section 5B.

A man of his words and deeds.   The neutral attitude of the *chün-tzu* is related to Confucius' special emphasis on the harmony of words and deeds. If morality deals with the relations between men, as the character *"jên"* suggests, living in accordance with *jên* morality requires the knowledge of men. And "without knowing *the force of* words, it is impossible to know men" (XX.3). Thus the harmony of words and deeds is a frequent theme of Confucian ethics. A *chün-tzu* must act in accordance with what he professes (VII.32). Even Confucius claimed he was not a *chün-tzu* in this sense: "In letters I am perhaps equal to other men, but *the character* of the superior man, carrying out in his conduct what he professes, is what I have not yet attained to" (VII.32). This doctrine of words and deeds, to borrow a phrase from Austin, may be said to be a case of "suiting the action to the word."[10] This sort of action, in real life, is formidable to accomplish, not only because of the difficult strength of character required, but also because of the dynamic diversity of human situations that vary a great deal in their normative import. To preserve a *chün-tzu's* freedom to adopt to changing and varying circumstances, Confucius laid more stress on the importance of suiting one's words to action. Thus Confucius remarked that a *chün-tzu* "acts before he speaks, and afterwards speaks according to his actions" (II.13; also IV.22; XIV.21). He is "modest in his speech but exceeds in his actions" (XIV.29). Ideally, a morally correct speech corresponds to a morally correct performance. A *chün-tzu* therefore does not engage in moral discourse for its own sake. He attempts to *suit* his words to actions performed. Conversely, his actions must, in other cases, conform to his words. This is particularly true of evaluative labels that others give him. He must live up to his title of being a *chün-tzu* (IV.5). Our present discussion is intimately related to the famous Confucian doctrine of rectification of *names (cheng ming),* for words of honor and morality have their normative import. The names of titles of persons and their roles in society pragmatically imply certain obligatory types of actions as befitting these names. To rectify names (*ming*) or moral words is to conform in action to the normative implications of these names.[11]

The notion of correct speech and action is important in Confucian ethics, not only for conduct in accordance with *jên* morality, but also for the successful execution of moral intentions within the form of a cultural life style (*li*). Moral words and action are embedded in ritual contexts. The significance of this *performative* aspect of *li* has been emphasized by Fingarette. In stressing this aspect of *li*, he brings the Confucian view closer to the Austinian insight on the significance of the forces of speech acts.[12] It is the *chün-tzu*, as previously mentioned, who is aware of the forces of speech. And from the standpoint of Confucian morality, a *chün-tzu* is a moral exemplar in both words and deeds. Suiting one's words to actions, of course, presupposes the satisfaction of the requirements of *jên* morality.

In sum, the notion of *chün-tzu* is Confucius' ideal of a paradigmatic individual which functions as a guiding standard for practical conduct. In Confucius' view ordinary moral agents may not attain sagehood (*sheng-jen*). However, they can look to a *chün-tzu* for guidance and may become *chün-tzu* themselves. The notion of *chün-tzu*, though an exemplary model for practical conduct, is not an ideal of a perfect man, but an ideal of a *superior man* who embodies the various qualities we have discussed.

B. Rules and Exceptions

One problematic feature in the preceding account relates to the *chün-tzu*'s neutrality or absence of commitment to specific courses of action. I have suggested that this neutral attitude is essential to one aspect of *i* (righteousness), i.e., to the exercise of judgment on the relevance of moral and ritual rules to concrete situations. However, *i* also has the plausible meaning of being a standard of righteousness. Confucius' remark on the neutrality of the *chün-tzu* in relation to *i* can thus be plausibly rendered in two different ways. In Legge's translation, which was quoted previously, the text runs: "The superior man (*chün-tzu*), in the world, does not set his mind either for anything or against anything; what is right (*i*) he will follow" (IV.10). The same text has been rendered by Chan as: "A superior man (*chün-tzu*) in dealing with the world is not for or against anything. He follows righteousness as a standard (*i*)." Legge's translation suggests the view that a *chün-tzu* does according to what he *thinks* is right in any circumstances in which he finds himself. His neutrality is, in this respect, a necessary prerequisite to his flexibility and adaptability to varying situations. In Chan's translation, the passage suggests the view that a *chün-tzu* does follow a moral standard but does not hold to any specific course of action prior to a judgment on the relevance of the moral standard. To hold righteousness as a standard is to hold fast to the Confucian moral point of view, for *i*, as we have seen, is contrasted with profit—a contrast that I regard as a contrast between morality and egoism. The two interpretations jointly are consistent with what I believe to be the plausible feature of Confucian ethics. And if this reconstructed account is correct, the Confucian moral point of view may be formally characterized as a morality of righteousness (the basic meaning of *i*) as contrasted with egoism, but understood in terms of the ideal of *jên*. A *chün-tzu* does what is right from the moral point of view in the sense of acting independently of personal interest or profit. However, adopting the Confucian point of view does not by itself dictate specific courses of action prior to an encounter with actual situations. The *chün-tzu*'s neutrality is his freedom of action, although this freedom is radically limited by the restraining orbits of his cultural life style (*li*). In other words, a *chün-tzu* remains free within the ritual scheme of conduct. He can succeed or fail to realize *jên* morality within this ritual universe.

However, there is also a sense of freedom in the *chün-tzu*'s judgment and interpretations of moral rules. In this regard, the *open texture* of moral rules is recognized in Confucian ethics. Moral and ritual rules retain their normative force in *normal* cases. But exigent circumstances may arise that alter their force or appropriateness. In commenting on Confucius' remark (IV.10), Chan instructively reminds us:

> This is a clear expression of both the flexibility and rigidity of Confucian ethics—flexibility in application but rigidity in standard. Here lies the basic idea of the Confucian doctrine of *Ching ch'uan*, or the standard and the exceptional, the absolute and the relative, or the permanent and the temporary. This explains why Confucius was not obstinate, had no predetermined course of action, was ready to serve or to withdraw whenever it was proper to do so, and according to Mencius, was a sage who acted according to the circumstance of the time.[13]

However, the doctrine of *ching ch'uan* rendered as the doctrine of "the standard and the exceptional" may be quite misleading. The relevant meaning of "*ching*" for our present purpose is an "invariable rule, a standard of conduct; constant, recurring"; that for *ch'uan*" is "exigency, circumstances; that which is irregular and opposed to *ching*, that which is constant or normal—from this comes, therefore, the idea of temporary, etc."[14] The doctrine of *ching ch'uan* can also be interpreted, more plausibly and significantly for moral philosophy, as a doctrine of the *normal* and the *exigent,* or the normal and the exceptional. We may speak of "the normal," from the moral point of view, as a rule that regularly and invariably applies to situations or actions that fall within the scope of its application. From this point of view, moral rules must be regularly observed for them to have the force of normative rules. This regularity is tied to their application to normal and clear-cut cases. The notion of *ching,* in effect, points to an aspect of our moral experience—the aspect of stability. Moreover, in real life one may confront situations that appear to fall outside the scope of the application of rules. These situations may be termed "abnormal" or "exigent" situations. *Ch'uan* focuses on such cases.

We may now apply this version of the doctrine of *ching ch'uan* to two perplexing passages in the works of Mencius.[15] The King Hsuan of Chi asked Mencius, "May a minister put his sovereign to death?" Mencius replied:

> He who outrages the benevolence (*jên*) *proper to his nature* is called a robber; he who outrages righteousness (*i*) is called a ruffian. The robber and ruffian we call a mere fellow. I have heard of the cutting off of the fellow Chau, but I have not heard of the putting a sovereign to death, *in his case.*

Legge comments on this passage that "killing a sovereign is not necessarily rebellion nor murder."[16] This is, no doubt, Mencius' point. But this sounds like double-talk, unless we understand the force of the implicit rule "Do not kill sovereign." Mencius' point seems to be that this rule does not apply to a case of this sort. The rule is judged to be irrelevant. When a person with the name (*ming*) or title of "sovereign" outrages *jên* and *i,* he is no longer deserving of that title. Here "sovereign" is an evaluative term. In the discourse, the sovereign is stripped of his *name.* To be a sovereign is to live up to what the *name* implies, to the requirements of *jên* and *i.* In this discourse of Mencius we do not have a case of exception to a rule, but rather a judgment, or, better, a ruling that the implicit rule does not apply to this sort of case. This ruling may function as a rule in future cases of the same sort, as Mencius seems to suggest in his view on the justification of revolution.

Reflections on another passage in Mencius, quite disturbing to logically minded readers, will perhaps bring out the doctrine more clearly. The discourse runs as follows:

> Shun-yu Kwan said, "Is it the rule that male and female shall

not allow their hands to touch in giving or receiving anything?"
Mencius replied, "It is the rule." Kwan asked, "If a man's sister-
in-law be drowning shall he rescue her with his hands?" Mencius said, "He who would not so rescue a drowning woman is a
wolf. For males and females not to allow their hands to touch in
giving or receiving is the *general rule* (*li*); when a sister-in-law is
drowning, to rescue her with the hand is a *peculiar exigency*
(*ch'uan*)."[17]

What Legge translates as "general rule" is actually the word "*li.*" It
would be better rendered in this discourse as "a ritual rule." Note that
in this discourse, a ritual rule is explicitly stated. The sort of situation is
also described quite clearly. Mencius did not recommend in the present
case that we break the rule, but rather that we act according to *ch'uan*
or the exigency of the situation. An exigent situation is a situation that
demands urgent and swift attention. It is a pressing situation that calls
for behavior appropriate to the circumstance. To regard a situation as
exigent does not necessarily imply that we are called upon to revise our
rule by making an exception to it. Rather, we are to attend to what the
situation demands. The situation may be said to be *exceptional* in the
sense that it does not appear to be covered by our normal application
of the rule. It is an exception to the rule only in the sense that the rule
apparently deemed relevant does not apply to the situation of this sort.
Thus we are in effect making a *ruling*. Mencius could have said, analogous to the first discourse examined, that we do not *call* that situation
of saving a drowning woman "touching hand" at all. The rule forbid-
ding males and females from touching hands applies to men and
women in normal social intercourse but does not extend to the situation in question. A ruling of this sort may be a guiding paradigm for
future situations.

   In discussing the doctrine of *ching ch'uan* we have implicitly utilized
an interpretation of the classic Confucian doctrine of rectifying names
(*cheng ming*) as a doctrine of calling things (i.e., objects, actions, persons,
and events) by right names. This interpretation is close to Austin's
remark that among the many questions that need to be asked on what
it is to do something, "we need to ask how we decide what is the *correct
name* for 'the' action that somebody did—what indeed, are the rules for
the use of 'the' action and the like."[18] I believe that this same point is
what the doctrine of rectification of names is designed to emphasize.
We need to see this doctrine in light of *ching ch'uan*, of the distinction
between the normal and the exigent. What is normally done requires

no justification. Only the exigent situation demands justification. More-over, the exigent situation is an abnormal one that requires a rectification of names or a prior decision on the "proper names" or "correct descriptions" before any attempt at a reasonable assessment of actions in terms of normative rules. To call actions by their right names is to do justice to exigent situations that do not occur with ready labels for proper identification or description. The decision or ruling on the "nature" of action is thus essential to the freedom of the moral agent who respects his moral practice. In a non-Confucian legalistic morality, the ruling is bound to be regarded as a "built-in" exception to a rule, thus giving rise to the problem of moral rules and exceptions. We shall pursue this theme in the following chapter.

This emphasis on the significance of ruling is, I think, one major contribution of Confucian ethics. In Confucian ethics, there is no straightforward application of moral and ritual rules. There are neither "rules of relevance" nor "rules of inference" for concrete moral performance.[19] For pedagogical purposes, we teach a body of rules, but in the dynamic situations of human life, we need to make rulings even in the absence of given rules. This is the logic of *chün-tzu*. A *chün-tzu* is an exemplary moral agent who embodies *jên* and *li*. He is a paradig-matic guide for ordinary moral agents by virtue of his ability to cope with the changing circumstance within the Confucian moral point of view. His neutrality of attitude toward specific courses of action pre-serves his freedom of action. The significance of the Confucian notion of *chün-tzu* thus lies in its suggestion of a conception of a reasonable moral agent who lives within a common way of life. A *chün-tzu* is thus a paradigmatic individual, an example of a creative moral agent within a moral practice. In the following chapter, we discuss creative agency within a moral practice independent of Confucian ethics. However, some of the features of our discussion depend on the plausibility of the distinction between normal and exigent situations.

C. Confucian and Other Moral Practices

This and the preceding chapter set forth the main normative content in which the Confucian notion of paradigmatic individuals, or *chün-tzu*, may be understood. What we termed the internal and external criteria, *jên* and *li*, are in effect intrinsic to a proper characterization of the Confucian moral point of view. A *chün-tzu* is an exemplary embodiment of this point of view in actual conduct. Although different moral practices do not possess equivalent appraisive concepts, it may be evident to a bilingual and bicultural agent that some concepts in two different appraisive languages or vocabularies do exhibit a similarity in the role they play in these moral practices. So in spite of the difficulty of translating appraisive concepts from one language to another, as incisively illustrated in Aschenbrenner's *Concepts of Value,* it is possible, for the purpose of understanding moral practices, to regard certain appraisive concepts as functionally equivalent concepts, thus allowing a speaker or writer to explain one moral concept in one language in terms of another concept in another language. This, of course, does not solve the problem of indeterminacy of translation. But it does provide a ground for justifying the importance of the comparative study of moral concepts that are *functionally equivalent* in different moral practices. In context, it is quite illuminating to translate *"jên"* as "benevolence" or "perfect goodness" or "human-heartedness." The last rendering in particular displays an affinity with the notion of benevolence as consideration and regard for other persons. The notion of functional equivalence of concepts, I believe, is implicit in William James' discussion on the "Moral Equivalence of War." James says, "I spoke of the 'moral equivalent' of war. So far, war has been the only force that can discipline a whole community, and until an equivalent discipline is organized, I believe that war must have its way."[20] This, of course, is not a plea for militaristic society, but an insistence on a functional equivalent for war that can take its place in communal discipline. James is speaking within a moral practice. The insight, however, does have a peculiar relevance to present-day moral turmoil within and around the peoples of the world.[21]

If our discussion of Confucian ethics is deemed intelligible and adequate, it points to an exciting task for moral philosophers as embracing within its enterprise of epistemology of morals an investigation into the possibility of functionally equivalent moral concepts in different cultural ways of life with distinctive vocabularies of appraisal. This task entails the recognition of a sort of moral relativity but does not necessarily form the ground for ethical relativism. The search for functionally equivalent concepts does entail the acknowledgment that moral concepts belonging to different moral practices exhibit a difference in their tie to perhaps radically distinct constitutive content. Thus moral concepts belonging to different moral practices have different operative criteria for their application. The search for a universal set of principles of morality, characteristic of traditional ethical endeavor, could perhaps be construed more profitably as a search for functionally equivalent moral concepts or principles rather than as a rational or pure theoretical investigation with no regard to the behavior and actuating import of actual moral concepts in different practices. Although *jên,* as previously noted, cannot be construed as an equivalent of the concept of Christian love or benevolence, it does appear to have the same functional role to play in Confucian and Christian moralities. For one thing, both concepts address the interpersonal setting of human relations, and both contain a similar reference to a dimension of care or affection, thus addressing the necessity of the recognition of the importance of moral sensibility. Of course, the import, both cognitive and practical, varies radically in accordance with their associated beliefs and cultural life styles. The notion of *li,* we may also note, finds its functional affinity with Catholic Christian emphasis on rites in the conduct of the mass, for both *li* and the religious rites in question seem to appear to perform a similar function in the formal context of performance in which each sincere moral agent expresses, endorses or reconfirms, invokes, and celebrates his moral commitment or values. In this way a cultural life style may become an integral part of a morality. A comparative study of functionally equivalent moral concepts can in this way be an illuminating base in which to accommodate the moral differences between peoples belonging to distinct moral communities. This may result in a convergence of moral attitudes and principles that expresses a common tie to humanity. For a moral philosopher, a task still remains: to determine the indispensability of functionally equivalent moral concepts and build upon the result of this determination an adequate epistemology of morals. Perhaps the plea of classical British intuitionists, such as Richard Price, for the knowledge of ultimate and basic principles of conduct independent of particular moral practices is in part an insistence on the indispensability of some functionally equivalent principles.[22] Their dubious epistemology of intuition or a priori knowledge need not discourage moral philosophers from the important task in the search for functionally equivalent moral concepts and principles. I suggest that the task, whether construed as a meta-ethical or metamoral exploration, remains a promising path on which to build an adequate epistemology of morals, i.e., in the search for justifying and explaining the second-order principles that determine the indispensability of certain functionally equivalent principles.

6

Moral Rules and Rulings

Throughout the preceding discussion the importance and centrality of the notion of ruling in understanding moral creativity have been stressed. A *ruling,* on our conception, is a decision or judgment on the relevance of rules to particular circumstances. We have, in particular, appealed to this notion in our account of Confucian ethics as an ethics of flexibility, exemplifying both the respect for a moral practice and the freedom of moral agents in the exercise of judgment in exigent situations. We now pursue this theme independently of Confucian ethics in considering the relationship between moral agents and moral practice, and the manner in which moral creativity may be further explored and elucidated.

A. Moral Practice

Our interest in the relevance of moral rules to creative agency within a moral practice necessitates a clearer statement of the notion of a moral practice. As was suggested in Chapter 1, a moral practice is a cultural way of life that may be characterized as a system of rules recognized as binding upon the conduct of a community of persons. This system of rules, or "ethical system," is in effect a cultural pattern that exemplifies "definite ideas regarding what constitutes right and wrong behavior in most situations involving social interaction with a high degree of consistency in the values which these ideas reflect." This conception, Linton continues, implies two propositions: (1) that "a large majority of its members accept this system consciously or otherwise," and (2) that "it is reflected in their normal, culturally patterned behavior."[1] A moral practice thus admits of a characterization from two different points of view. Hart reminds us that "when a social group has certain rules of conduct, this fact affords an opportunity for many closely related yet different kinds of assertion; for it is possible to be concerned with the rules, either merely as an observer who does not himself accept them, or as a member of the group which accepts and uses them as guides to conduct. We may call these respectively the 'external' and the 'internal' points of view."[2] These two different points of view reflect two different types of concern and interest. The external point of view stresses mainly an aspect of moral practice in terms of regularity and consistency of behavior. It implies no commitment to the regulative force of moral rules. The internal point of view, on the other hand, is the point of view of a moral agent who regards the moral rules as authoritative standards for criticism of deviation from the practice in question. These two points of view are distinct but not exclusive. It is a difference in emphasis. A social scientist more naturally adopts the external point of view, for his primary interest lies in the description of the behavioral pattern as subject to hypotheses and empirical confirmation. A phenomenologist of morals more appropriately adopts the internal point of view, for his interest lies primarily in understanding the phenomenal field of moral agency and performance. Consistent with our interest in understanding moral creativity or creativity of moral agents within a moral practice, we take the internal point of view.

From the internal point of view, we shall regard a *moral practice* (e.g., Confucian or Christian) as a communal form of activity characterized both by a set of moral rules which are regarded by the participants as binding upon their conduct, and by certain sanctions for deviant behavior.[3] This conception of a moral practice is admittedly less precise and formal than the technical one based on the game analogy, but it is more faithful to the open-textured characteristic of the moralities of various cultural groups.[4] Every living moral practice appears to be infected with this open texture or "possibility of vagueness."[5] This is in part evident in the nature of moral concepts or moral rules as *open* rather than complete notions. Whenever doubt occurs concerning the proper application of a rule, we seem unable to "fill up all the possible gaps" in any precise manner that is not subject to further emendation and dispute. The content of a moral rule remains vague and imprecise prior to a decision on its relevance to particular cases. Berkeley has noted this feature in his *Passive Obedience*. While defining a version of restricted utilitarianism, Berkeley admits that the precept "Thou Shalt Not Kill" does not have any precise content, "because it is expressed in too general terms. . . . In order to have a distinct declaration of it, either those general terms may be changed for others of a more limited sense, as *kill* for *murder,* or else, from the general proposition remaining in its full latitude, exceptions may be made of those precise cases which, not agreeing with the notion of murder, are not prohibited by the law of nature.[6]

Another reason in favor of our informal conception of a moral practice lies in the fact that few moralities familiar to modern men appear in a completely codified form with a determinate hierarchy of rules for the regulation and justification of conduct. With regard to any moral practice, a value theorist could perhaps raise a question concerning "the overall structure of mandatory values and disvalues."[7] This sort of question undoubtedly serves our theoretical systematic purpose, i.e., in the systematic construction of a sort of value hierarchy. But from the *position* of a reflective moral agent within a particular moral practice, the question of a normative hierarchy of rules remains a constant concern because of the shifting scenes of conditions that confront the agent. Any theoretically preestablished hierarchy is always subject to the agent's critical reconsideration of its import to his own life, his ideals, and his aspirations. For this reason, we shall regard the rules, like the Decalogue, as forming an open or indeterminate set in which various orderings in terms of import are possible for moral agents. In Christian morality, for instance, "Love thy neighbor as thyself" may be taken by one moral agent as the basic and ultimate rule of conduct, and the other rules as deriving their force or import from this basic rule. On the other hand, another agent may take "Love the Lord, thy God," as a basic or superordinate rule in which all the other rules are deemed subsumable. In a similar way, Confucian morality, described in terms of rules governing *jên* (human-heartedness) and *li* (propriety), may be conceived by different agents as having different import. In this sense, within a common moral practice, an observer may witness a diversity of moral judgments due to the varying personal import of moral rules for different moral agents.

In the language of the current distinction between moral principles and moral rules, we may characterize this diversity in terms of the relative dependency of moral principles upon the judgments and character of moral agency. What is a principle to one agent may be a rule to another. In abstraction from the life and character and judgments of individual moral agents, we may say that "whereas rules are more specific and concrete, principles are more general and abstract. Principles are involved in the justification and clarification of rules, and both are involved in determining the morality of conduct."[8] This distinction would be a relative one in the context of moral agency, for what is taken as a principle or rule depends on how the agent views his moral practice in terms of its significance for his life. Should we want to make the distinction between moral rules and principles, we could use the notion of principles in the sense of a person *having principles.* As Kovesi points out, " 'Being a principle' is not a feature of statements or judgments. It is people—and only some people—who make and have principles, or live according to principles."[9] Thus we may speak of a moral agent as having principles. These principles may be identical with the rules in his moral practice. But it is possible for the moral agent to comply with rules without adopting them as principles in the sense of personal rules of conduct that are constitutive of and significant for his moral life. Insofar as rules are regarded as principles, these rules will have a peculiar personal import. In this way, the moral rules embedded within a moral practice are candidates competing for admission into the domain of a man's moral principles.

Hare's terminology of "decision of principle" appears to be a felicitous term for designating this conception of moral principles. For in the proposed conception, I, as a moral agent, can be said to accept, adopt, or decide to accept or adopt a moral rule as a principle constitutive of my life. Of course, the rules in my moral practice, in their social and intersubjective function, are not matters of decision insofar as I live with others in a cultural and communal setting. The moral rules compel acceptance insofar as I am a member of a moral community. But if the question on the sense of being a person *qua* person is deemed meaningful, my compliance with rules does not logically entail my acceptance of them as my principles—they may not have an intrinsic import in the personal-valuational sense. For moral rules to become part of a person's principles they must be accepted as in some sense definitive of the person's way of life. In this sense, within a moral practice there can be a diversity of moral principles characteristic of various individual ways of life.

In spite of the diversity of the import of a moral practice for different agents, a moral practice has both a *de facto* and *de jure* force. The *de facto* force consists in the agent's recognition of his moral practice as having certain obligatory requirements, the violation of which may bring about unwanted consequences. The *de jure* force results from the agent's acknowledgment of the *de facto* moral practice as binding upon his conduct. In this way, a moral practice has both a power and an authority for moral agents.

B. *Creativity within a Moral Practice*

The conception of a moral practice expounded in the preceding section raises a question concerning the nature of creativity within a moral practice. Preliminary to a clarification of this question, we must take note of the recent emphasis in moral philosophy on the logic of moral concepts and reasoning. This epistemological interest in the *formal* aspect of moral practices in terms of universalizability of moral judgments does shed light upon the claim to rationality that appears to be implicit in moral practices in general. The question of moral creativity, however, deals essentially with the *material* aspect of moral practice. It is a question concerning the substance or content of a morality. A reflective exploration of this question within the internal point of view of a moral practice may be construed as a task in the logic of application rather than in the logic of moral reasoning.[10]

It is a common view that *moral principles,* in our sense of basic and superordinate rules of conduct, perform two related roles from the internal point of view.[11] "We appeal to them either for justification or guidance in face, say, of challenge or of doubt," and they "serve to organize and unify a whole range of phenomena which we could otherwise make no sense of at all."[12] Our question on moral creativity may in part be formulated in the retrospective point of view, i.e., in terms of the nature of appeal to *principles* within a given practice. If the *moral principles* of any given practice are used for justification of rules, and rules are in turn justificatory of actions, what is the notion of justification involved in this process of appeal? To what are we appealing when we speak of the justificatory function of *moral principles?* Or, more generally, what sense of moral creativity is intelligible in speaking of a particular moral practice?

If we grant that *moral principles* are essentially open textured in the sense that their application depends on interpretations of the agents within a given moral practice, the notion of moral justification cannot be understood apart from the way *moral principles* are interpreted in actual moral deliberation. If a moral practice, say, contains such *principles* enjoining promise keeping or benevolence, such *principles* (admittedly regulative in function), being open textured, are void of specific content. As Hare succinctly states, "The general end or principle is vacuous until by our detailed instruction we have given it content."[13] But we must note that even if our instruction is detailed and meticulous, the learner must apply and interpret. Take the *principle* of benevolence: if it is recognized as a constitutive element of a given moral practice, apart from its practical context of application, the principle says very little about the nature of benevolent actions or how one should go about classifying benevolent and nonbenevolent acts; it says practically nothing as to what extent conformity to this principle is praiseworthy and to what degree the violation of this *principle* is blameworthy. In spite of this, for all practical purposes, the *principle* of benevolence is considered to have fairly definite content, or at least ordinary men and moral philosophers speak of the *principle* as if it possessed some sort of content and substantive meaning. How then do we resolve this apparent paradox: that *moral principles* are essentially regulative or directives to conduct, and at the same time they require interpretation or appear to provide no definitive answers to practical problems as they confront moral agents?

The preceding paradox may be resolved by a distinction between the *minimum* and *maximum* content of *moral principles.* If *moral principles* are essentially open textured, still, in applying them, the moral agents are guided by what they regard as acceptable interpretations. From an internal point of view of a moral practice, this minimum content is provided by the background of moral teaching presupposing a common understanding of what these *principles* are meant to apply to. In other words, moral agents are taught some precepts by way of examples, which constitute the guiding interpretations of *moral principles.* These precepts, on the whole, are not consciously formulated in different societies. They may appear in proverbial forms, more like counsels of prudence than imperatives of morality. They form the common understanding of the functions of *moral principles* within a given practice. But this use requires an individual act of interpretation to give the principles their maximum content—maximum in the sense of a satisfactory and adequate relevance to particular situations. Thus in applying the preexisting *principles* or moral rules in general, we are giving them their maximum meaning in the more precise delineation of their scope of application in concrete situations. Moreover, the maximum content of *moral principles* in some actual situations may also become a sort of *minimum* content of the same *principles* in future situations. The maximum content may be described in terms of the individual's rulings that *reconstitute* the content of his moral practice. The content of a morality is therefore not static but changing, owing to the diverse interpretations of *moral principles* or moral rules in general. As Pole very clearly states, "Morality is not a single concept clearly defined: we rather find a growing tangle of fibres that overlap, branch, and join again; and to pick out any single strand seems merely arbitrary."[14]

Viewed in terms of the distinction between minimum and maximum content of *moral principles,* the notion of justification appears to be an internal process of appeal to the minimum content of *moral principles.* Since *moral principles* are open textured, particular instances of appeal to them for justification would seem to be instances of ascription of maximum content. Thus implicit in the appeal to *moral principles* is a notion of ruling or moral creativity. To what extent an agent's departure from the minimum content of *moral principles* may be said to be justified remains a question for further exploration. In Section 6E, we pursue this question in terms of rulings and justification. At this juncture, we only take note of the importance of the shift from the internal to the external point of view of a moral practice. Such a shift within the context of moral agency seems to be accomplished only when moral agents introduce different interpretations to *moral principles.* The minimum content, or the established meanings, of *moral principles* may on reflection turn out to be totally inadequate in their application to concrete situations that beset moral agents in perhaps radically individual settings. The moral agents may need to shift from an internal to an external point of view. Once this shift is accomplished, the minimum content of *moral principles* will no longer appear an authoritative guide and may have to be progressively enlarged or modified to embrace new situations and persons; or it may have to be replaced or assigned a subordinate status, thereby giving scope for other moral rules for occupying a more prominent role of ascending importance within the moral practice.

Detached from his own peculiar individual setting, a moral agent may in this way act as a critic of a moral practice or as a social reformer. The minimum content of a moral practice may in part become a topic of critical consideration. The moral agent's role here is perhaps not unlike a judicial reviewer of legal decisions and principles, who asks external questions not in the interest of mere observation or in a more adequate description of the functioning of a legal system, but in the interest of advocating change in legal rules. However, within the individualized setting of a moral agent, concerning his own predicament, the shift from the internal to external point of view will probably be a momentary rather than an enduring affair. His activity here is perhaps not unlike that of a translator engaged in translating a particular sentence from one language to another with a view of preserving the *sense* or meaning of that sentence. Much of the difficulty does not lie in the reference or denotation of the terms, but in communicating in another language the sense of the sentence in the original text. At the end, the translator must decide on one rendering that he thinks is relatively adequate to the meaning of the sentence, fully conscious that the translation may be challenged by other translators equally competent in handling the languages in question. His decision or ruling is therefore subject to further criticism by others. So also with the rulings of individual moral agents that concern primarily his own problematic setting. They are subject to challenge and criticism by his fellow agents, particularly when his rulings are generalized and detached from their original habitat of personal predicament. There are no self-certifying rulings. Apart from their original personal contexts, each ruling on the maximum content of *moral principles* is a subject of critical consideration.

The distinction between *minimum* and *maximum* content of *moral principles* or moral rules in general may be more felicitously termed the *constitutive* and *reconstitutive* content of a moral practice. In what follows, we use the latter terminology to focus on rulings as acts of reconstituting the content of a moral practice.

C. Acceptance, Assurance, and Construction

We now turn to a more general characterization of the relationship between a moral agent and his moral practice, in particular, the manner in which moral creativity may be elucidated in terms of the notion of ruling. We may conceive the relation between a moral agent and his practice in terms of three attitudes, not necessarily incompatible, and corresponding activities of moral agency. We shall call these activities moral *acceptance, assurance,* and *construction.* As implied in our conception of moral practice, the attitude of acceptance may be determined by the degree of strength of assent to the moral rules. Ideally, a full acceptance of a moral rule of the form "One ought to do x" implies that the agent "always obeys this moral rule," and "that his obedience is unconditional in the sense that it is to be explained by reference to the rule."[15]

In real life, few moral agents accept moral rules as principles in this strong sense, because of varying situations and what may be termed "personal valuational factors," i.e., considerations of import to moral agents that are not explicitly or implicitly recognized by the moral practice. Whatever his degree of strength of acceptance, the agent's attitude signifies the initial acceptability and applicability of the moral rules. Actions in accordance with moral rules have thus a performatory or commissive character. This initial attitude need not commit the moral agent to viewing all his actions as subsumable under a given set of rules, unless the rules themselves are always judged as relevant to actual situations. But since the moral rules are open textured, a reflective agent may take a critical stance toward his practice. Where the moral rules function in *normal* circumstances, the agent may be said to apply his rules in a straightforward manner. His judgment may be described in deductive form. Thus, in normal situations, the rules are applied without question. Situations that are recognized as instances for the application of moral rules are deemed to be *rule determinate*. When such normal situations occur, the moral agent may be said to be *assured* of his acceptance of his moral practice.[16] In this sense, moral rules function as sorting devices by classifying situations into various types. *Moral assurance* may be regarded as a confirmation of a moral practice from the agent's point of view. In this way a moral practice is strengthened and may be said to be warranted in the continuous and unquestioned application of the rules to actual situations. The constitutive content of the moral practice remains stable. The situations are viewed as *normal* in the sense that rules regularly operate without giving rise to doubts or uncertainty. Wittgenstein says, "When I obey a rule, I do not choose. I obey the rule blindly."[17] In normal situations where I merely comply with a rule, I do not reflect upon the question "What ought I to do?" Thus mere compliance with a moral rule does not strictly raise any question of application, or of choice between alternative courses of action. Applying a rule, unlike mere compliance, is thus not a case of blind obedience, but of an intelligent performance within the *de jure* setting of a moral practice.

However, in cases where the situations confronted by the moral agent are deemed by him to be *abnormal,* the possibility is open to the agent to exercise his judgment on the relevance and meaning or interpretation of moral rules. Since moral rules are open textured, they stand there like "signposts," leaving occasions for doubt and uncertainty.[18] A moral rule does not therefore dictate its own application. In these cases of doubt, when situations are judged to be abnormal, the agent faces a problematic predicament. The situation may be such that conflicting rules *seem* to be relevant simultaneously, thus issuing incompatible requirements. Or a situation may arise which is not clearly covered by the moral rules, thus calling for an individual decision. The constitutive content of the moral practice does not issue clear guidance. Philosophers since Kant have concentrated more on situations where there is a "conflict of duties," and less on the relevance of rules to novel situations. However we characterize these situations of uncertainty in detail, two different, but not exclusive, strategies are available to moral agents. Both these strategies depict the constructive character of moral agency. Assuming that an agent adopts a critical attitude toward moral rules, one strategy in dealing with uncertain and abnormal situations may be depicted as that of construing moral rules as *general rules* which have *exceptions* in varying circumstances.[19] The *creative* aspect of moral agency is then understood as a constructive activity which the agent performs in modifying and qualifying rules in terms of exceptions in different situations. Thus a judgment of, or decision on, the relevance of a rule, which we have termed a "ruling," is in effect an extension or delimitation of the scope of applicability of the rules in terms of either range of situations or range of persons.

It has been pointed out that "in justifying an exception one is actually justifying a class of exceptions, and is thus, in effect, modifying the understanding of the original rule by restricting its scope." A restriction of scope is thus designed to cope with conflicting requirements of moral rules in particular instances.[20] In uncertain situations where no rule is obviously applicable, however, the agent may extend the rule to the situation instead of making an arbitrary decision. In both types of case, the agent may appeal to the spirit or intent of the rules in making rulings, thus converting an indeterminate situation into a rule-determinate one.

The foregoing strategy for dealing with uncertain situations need not assume that moral rules have recognized or built-in exceptions.[21] This assumption is legitimate only when one construes existing moral rules as functioning like legal rules with exempting conditions, as noted by Berkeley (see Section 6A). This would be true only if we were dealing with a "closed" or codified moral practice. It is doubtful whether such an assumption applies to all moral practices. In Confucian morality, for instance, it is very difficult to ascribe any notion of a rule as having recognized exceptions. All moral rules, particularly those in ritual form, are precise and specific. They do not allow for exceptions in any recognizable sense. And yet, were he to view the resolution of uncertain situations in terms of the language of rules, a Confucian agent would probably make such situations exceptions *to* the rules. Making an exception to a rule would constitute a ruling. The ruling in this sense would be an act of adjusting a set of rules to changing circumstances, rather than a prior determination of the character of individual problems and situations.

The view that moral rules have built-in exempting conditions is also problematic, for the application of moral rules depends on the ordinary capacity of the moral agents to comply with them, and this in turn depends on the rules having a manageable complexity. The ordinary man has to apply and interpret his moral practice "without recourse to a Supreme Court or House of Lords."[22] In construing rules as having built-in exceptions, we in effect assume that these exceptions can be recognized and applied. But it is difficult for the moral agent to recognize these exceptions in all circumstances covered by the intended scope of the moral rules. If we assume that there are built-in exceptions, we must face the consequence of our rules having an unmanageable complexity, since these so-called exceptions ultimately rest on the agent's understanding of the constitutive content of his moral practice. It appears more plausible to account for the constitutive content of the moral practice in terms of the varying understanding of the moral agents. In making rulings in abnormal circumstances, the moral agents may have to act by *reconstituting* the content and import of moral rules. These rulings are bound to vary from one agent to another. There is no assurance that all moral agents would render the same judgment on the content of the moral rules in abnormal and uncertain situations.

What we have termed the first strategy for dealing with abnormal situations focuses upon ruling as an act of modifying or qualifying the function of an existing moral rule. The effect of this ruling is to regard moral rules as subject to revision to accommodate novel cases. The agent in question regards the existing moral rules as in principle general rules that can flexibly apply to uncertain cases. Here the agent is still operating within the confines of the moral practice. The ruling is made in light of the existing moral requirements, thus continuous with and consistent with the agent's prior understanding of the nature and content of rules within his moral practice. This continuous application of moral rules, in accordance with its constitutive content, gives us an understanding of the *stable* aspect of morality, for regularly and successfully applied rules in effect secure stability within a moral practice. In this way, rules tend to regularize human situations in the sense that they are in part intended to stabilize the changing scenes of morality. Rules, if successfully applied, thus establish the regularity of behavior. They define the *normality* of situations.

The first strategy thus assumes that understanding the function and content of a moral practice presupposes an ability to qualify rules in situations of uncertainty. What appears as an abnormal situation to an agent is a challenge to the exercise of such an ability. The ruling rendered, in effect, is intended to normalize the situation within the context of a body of moral rules. If we generalize this attitude, we may say that strictly speaking, there are no abnormal or exigent situations. In principle, a moral rule can be stretched to cover novel cases. And in this way the agent reconstitutes the content of the moral practice by incorporating his rulings within the operative scope of the established moral rules. Moral rules are regarded as subject to a variety of interpretations and rulings, but these reconstitutive acts must be regarded as satisfying the applicability conditions of the rules and not as an intrusion into the normal function of the moral practice. An agent, deploying the first strategy, remains faithful to his moral practice.

D. Creativity in Exigent Situations

Unlike the first strategy, the second strategy focuses on the character of the uncertain situation rather than on the constitutive content of the moral practice. An uncertain situation is thus an *exigent* situation that calls for decision and judgment quite independent of the requirements of the moral rules. On this view, uncertain situations are not items to be accommodated by existing rules, since they are by nature rule indeterminate. What is central to the second strategy is the assumption that uncertain situations, construed as a difference in the conception of problematic situations, depict a difference in focus. The one stresses the primacy of moral practice, the other the primacy of occurrent situations. The freedom of the moral agent to envisage alternative courses of action is always stressed by the second strategy. On this view, one may construe rules in a rigorous fashion as having no exceptions, thus regarding the given rules of a moral practice as having a prior determinate scope. This need not be an implausible construction of the nature of moral rules so long as one recognizes the price of their possible irrelevance. But the second strategy need not commit itself to a rigorous view of moral rules. It can be content to focus on the significance of moral pioneers or creative agents in the exercise of rulings that affect the content of a moral practice. Whether the agent recognizes a built-in exception or that a problematic situation is an exception to a rule, he exercises his judgment and ruling on the relevance of moral rules to particular circumstances. (See Section 5B for a discussion of this view as a central feature of Confucian ethics.)

The first strategy in effect points to one sort of ruling, the second strategy, on the other hand, regards the nature of rulings as an open question not prejudged by the prior force of an existing moral practice. It opens up a wider dimension of moral construction or creativity on the part of the moral agents. In this way, our prior understanding of the constitutive content of moral rules is always subject to individual transformation and reconstitution. Allowing this dimension of moral creativity within a moral practice gives us an understanding of the dynamic character of living moralities. Thus we may say, as individual reflective agents, that "all decisions except those, if any, that are completely arbitrary are to some extent decisions of principles. We are always setting precedents for ourselves."[23] The rulings that moral agents make amount to decisions or judgments that may guide their conduct in future cases similar to the problematic situations that gave rise to these rulings.

The two strategies available to moral agents within a moral practice amount, in the last analysis, to two sorts of ruling. We call these decisions and judgments of the relevance of moral rules to actual situations *rulings* in order to suggest an analogy with legal terminology. In the context of judicial decisions, the judge renders authoritative decisions or rulings on certain debated points of law. But unlike a judicial ruling, a ruling in the moral context is not automatically rendered authoritative. The authority of these rulings depends on the acceptance of other agents as relevant to their own problematic situations.

However, in regarding individual judgments and decisions as rulings, I mean to suggest that these rulings may acquire an authoritative force for the agent himself and his fellows when they are generally accepted as part of the constitutive content of the moral practice. Thus the rulings of certain individuals, particularly those whose lives exemplify the embodiment of a moral practice, may become the constitutive content of a moral practice, and so furnish a source for moral instruction in the understanding and enforcement of moral rules.

According to Wittgenstein, there are two ways in which one makes a move within a language game: "In the one case we make a move in an existent game, in the other we establish a rule of the game. Moving a piece could be conceived in these two ways: as a paradigm for future moves, or as a move in an actual game."[24] This suggestive remark seems an apt characterization of the two sorts of ruling revealed by the two strategies. In the first strategy, which aims at modifying a rule to accommodate a new case, the ruling can be conceived as a move within a moral practice. When a rule is thus modified the agent simply regards the uncertain situation at hand as a subsumptive case of the rule understood in light of the qualification. No question of doubt need arise, for the ruling can easily be made consistent with the constitutive content of the moral practice. The second strategy, which regards the uncertain situation as rule indeterminate, in effect attempts to establish a new rule. The ruling in question appears to have a twofold projective character. In the first the agent projects his ruling as "a paradigm for future moves." And for this sort of ruling to acquire a public significance, the agent must project his ruling as acceptable from the viewpoint common to other agents within the moral practice. But this projection of consensual acceptance cannot be assured, since other agents have the same discretion in the interpretation of relevance of rules to particular circumstances. As previously pointed out, any ruling is subject to further challenge and criticism. A moral practice thus involves both a consensual and a dissensual character. As Mayo points out, we must regard "the existence of disputes, controversies, and differences of opinions on moral principles as not merely something that has to do justice to the facts, but as very much more important: as something that actually makes morality what it is, and has to be a central feature of a moral theory."[25]

E. Rulings and Justification

In this section, we discuss different types of rulings and their justifications. In recent philosophy, it is almost an unquestioned assumption that justification of beliefs in general rests on certain accepted criteria, standards, or principles. Applying this model to ethics, moral actions are said to be justified or validated by an appeal to rules, and rules are justified by an appeal to principles or more basic rules. According to this conception, justification is an upward, vertical movement from the concrete situations to abstract rules or principles. In the case of justified rulings as stressed by the first strategy, a justification is a process of application of *moral principles* to rules or rules to actions and situations. Here the justified ruling is viewed essentially as a subsumptive process. Actions in accordance with moral rules have thus a retrospective character, in that they resemble a past deed by being of a determinate character describable in terms of the existing moral rules. Justification is a backward-looking process, for it refers back to the accepted rules as standards. But we must note here that the determinateness of the character of action is a matter of categorial characterization or description. It is formal rather than concrete and existential. As previously observed, this model of moral judgments indicates an interest in the historical continuity of a moral practice. The stability of the moral life is by and large secured by this dimension of moral judgments. This model of justification is a useful focal device for the aspect of stability of the moral life. However, if we admit into our reflection the instability of the world, we need to adopt a different perspective by seeing our moral rules as needing constant adjustment to the changing scenes of life. This emphasis is a major insight of John Dewey. But as reflective moral agents, we do not thereby surrender our historical interest in our moral practice.

In normal situations where actions fall under the scope of moral rules, our ruling on the relevance of these rules does not occupy the center of attention. Ruling like this is a subsumptive process. In this process our understanding of rules does not affect their application. Justification of rulings may be described as a deductive process. Where rulings occur without any explicit connection with our moral practice, to be moral, they are required to have some sort of contact with the *background* of the moral practice. The uses of moral concepts do in general presuppose a certain *form of life* that gives these concepts significance. Thus it has been claimed that concepts such as stealing, honesty, sincerity, murder, and treachery require certain kinds of background that give them intelligibility.[26] As Wittgenstein remarks, "What has to be accepted, the given, is—so one could say— forms of life."[27] In ruling or judging the relevance of a certain rule to a particular circumstance, we in effect establish a specific *context* of action. On the one hand, the ruling, so to speak, establishes a *tie* between the moral practice and concrete situations; on the other, it establishes the *tie* between the practice and the background. In general, we may regard the background of a moral practice as a reservoir of possible contexts for moral judgment. The context of a judgment is selective, in some sense, of the relevant features that lie in the background. Contexts are *field dependent* in the sense that the background provides the field upon which relevant considerations may be drawn. The field or background furnishes an operative boundary for acting to which the contexts are partial specifications. Contexts are the lines we draw in particular cases. The appeal to moral rules for justification is parasitic upon selective contexts. We seldom speak of the contexts of judgments; since the contexts are assumed to be relevant, they are taken for granted in our judgments. That is why the articulation of the contexts may be subject to disagreement. The disagreement may be resolved by an appeal to larger or *wider* contexts. In so doing we are attempting to draw from our background more relevant features for consideration. The contexts may be wide or narrow depending on the nature of the disagreement. The rules that we use are subject to the ruling in terms of the various features of the background that form the immediate contexts of judgment and decision. Thus in simple cases, rules are applied by way of subsuming individual cases. In complicated cases, as in those of apparently relevant conflicting rules, we have to make a judgment of the context—a ruling based on understanding the background as subject to articulation in particular cases.

We may regard the background of a moral practice as an inchoate form of life to which contexts for judgments and decision and actions are the selective articulations. We do not in practice attempt to articulate and specify the form of life *in toto*. Our attempt to do so would be bound to be abstract and trivial since the total articulation, if it is at all possible, would deprive the background of its life. To specify the background *in toto* would be analogous to the attempt to specify the totality of one's intentions in the contexts of doing. This total specification would be trivial, for it converts a form of life to a book of rules of life. But a book of rules of life cannot take care of the contingency and complexity of a moral life.

The lack of a need to specify *in toto* our background is in part the reason for the senselessness of speaking of choosing one's own form of life. For choice, if it is conscious, would involve the total articulation of this background in terms of a series of propositions. The form of life, however, is not a series of propositions to be stated but is more like the reservoir of personal intentions, the orbit that provides intelligibility to our moral reasons and actions. Living cannot be converted to a propositional function. The moral world in which we act, suffer, and enjoy is a lived world, not an architectonic construction of our intellect.

As moral agents in a community we all live in light of our background insofar as we *agree* in our responses to moral problems and considerations. As Wittgenstein pointed out: "That agreement is not an agreement in opinions but in a form of life."[28] We do not choose what is to count as a moral consideration since what makes a consideration moral can only be intelligible in light of the agreement in a form of life.[29] To be intelligible, the rulings we make in particular circumstances must therefore presuppose a dependence upon the field of our moral background. They are, in this way, *field-dependent* judgments. This field-dependent character points to normal anchorage of public significance in the sense of universality and objectivity that are characteristic of much of our moral judgments that bespeak their tie to a social life. Morality in this sense is a communal affair. However, rulings, particularly those in exigent circumstances, are directed primarily to the problematic situations that beset the moral agents. They are in this way *situation dependent,* for it is the particular uncertain situations that give rise to their urgency and necessity. The situation-dependent character of rulings marks the domain of reasonableness of decisions and actions. In order not to be an arbitrary agent, the individual must act according to "right reason," as stressed by Aristotle. But such a manner of acting is not subject to a general description, for we are not dealing with fixed data that can be organized in terms of formulas or recipes for resolving problems. And when we come to treating particular problems, our discussion is bound to be imprecise, "since these do not come under the heading of any art that can be transmitted by precept, but the agent must consider on each different occasion what the situation demands."[30] What is reasonable in a particular situation does not admit of discussion in terms of canons. As Anscombe remarked, "There can in principle be *no canon* other than giving a few examples."[31] The examples perhaps can be given in terms of the paradigmatic rulings of certain individuals who seem to have a perceptive insight into what is required in particular exigent circumstances. However, "what is reasonable" remains a floating notion that seems to be related to *timeliness,* or what is the fitting and appropriate thing to do in a situation. This is a characteristic feature of *chün-tzu* in Confucian ethics. It is a very difficult notion to explain with any degree of clarity. Perhaps the notion of timeliness, incidentally a pervasive notion in the Confucian classic *I Ching,* may be understood in terms of Austin's term "suiting words to actions," as suggested in the discussion of *chün-tzu* in Chapter 5. The point of reasonableness is the suiting of our moral rules to exigent situations. *Prima facie,* any situation may have a nature that is not rule determinate. Situations in human life do not occur with ready labels for identification or proper names or descriptions. To determine them by rule descriptions or "suiting the situations to the words" is one way of describing situations, but this is not the only way.

That is why our notion of timeliness is an open notion, since any situation is "open" to alternative descriptions in accordance with the rulings of particular moral agents. None can claim to be an essential description independent of the appreciation of the problems that beset particular moral agents. When rulings are also seen to be field dependent, they have a significance in preserving the continuity of a moral practice. The field-dependent and situation-dependent character of rulings, taken together, point to the possible dynamic continuity of a moral practice. Rulings, in our sense, are experiments in paradigmity. When such experiments are deemed successful, they become part of the constitutive content of a moral practice.

To justify rulings completely is to do justice to both their field-dependent and situation-dependent character. It is, however, very difficult, and perhaps theoretically impossible, to formulate a theory of justification here. For to propose such a theory is in effect to propose a theory on the criteria of relevance. But if we have such a set of criteria of relevance we do not need the notion of ruling stressed in our discussion. Ruling, particularly in exigent situations, is an art that is not governed by logical canons. It is justified more in the sense of *reasonableness,* as befitting particular circumstances within a moral practice. But unlike *rationality,* reasonableness is more a form of Aristotelian practical wisdom that seems to be existentially characteristic of some moral persons rather than an abstract property of the moral life.

The two strategies we characterized in Sections 6C and 6D may be conceived in terms of a divergence of two approaches employed by *rational* and *reasonable* moral agents. The first strategy is essentially the approach of a theorist. It may be called a *logical approach* in that "the primary concern is to resolve beforehand all the difficulties and problems which can arise in the most varied situations, which one tries to imagine, by applying the rules, laws, and norms one is accepting."[32] This is the approach of the rational man who aims at a systemic coherence of rules and situations by attempting to fit all situations and actions into a manageable set of formulas. His attitude toward exigent situations treats situations as amenable to description and classification in terms of existing moral concepts. Exigent situations are therefore items that call for classification in terms of his moral principles. These novel cases are thus viewed as built-in exceptions intended by the moral rules. They have no integrity of their own. A *reasonable* moral agent is more likely to be a man of action who exercises rulings in exigent situations. He would "resolve problems as they arise" and "rethink his concepts and rules in terms of real situations and of the decisions required for action."[33] In this way he preserves his freedom of judgment and action in order to cope with unforeseen and unexpected circumstances in his life. He will not and need not minimize the importance of moral rules in normal situations, but preserves his sense of freedom of ruling on the relevance of rules to particular exigent situations. If we view moral rules as essentially "rules of inference," the reasonable man would probably insist on the pointlessness of formulating criteria of relevance, since if there are such criteria, they are still dependent on occasional rulings rather than on an a priori determination of their concrete relevance to conditions of his life.

If the preceding remarks on reasonable rulings are deemed clear, they do not offer an answer to the puzzling question "How does an agent recognize or know what is or is not fitting to his situation?" For normal situations, the agent can answer the question by citing appropriate rules. For exigent situations, the question cannot be answered except perhaps in giving a sort of retrospective story of the sorts of considerations that influence the agent's judgment on what the situation requires as an appropriate action. There appears to be no need to appeal to intuition to settle any query. The agent can be challenged for his judgment and action that issues from it. To justify his ruling in exigent situations is in effect to *vindicate* himself, to clear away any suspicion of a wrong or arbitrary action. To vindicate himself, the agent may point out that *his* ruling and corresponding action are what the exigent situation demands as an appropriate action in the sense that an examination of the nature of the situation leaves him no choice between alternatives. The ruling is the only "permissible move" to make within the context of the situation. The agent can be mistaken about this, for his retrospective account of the features involved in the situation may be incomplete, or he may have included in his judgment some features of the situation which possess no moral import or relevance. The process of vindicating oneself in discourse is more a dialogic process, i.e., an *open* discourse that may well involve a wide range of factors not readily captured in some predetermined set of logical canons or criteria of relevance. The acceptability of a piece of vindication depends on the nature of the particular audience at issue. We would here expect the reasonable agent to engage in discursive vindication, for this appears to be the only recourse for showing the nonarbitrary character of his rulings. If this observation is correct, we may raise a further question on the nature of discursive vindication. On this question the conative-affective factors that affect the agent's ruling are likely to have a significant role to play. So also some notion of an appeal to reflective desirability of the agent's points at issue is likely to be involved. This suggestion opens up a facet of moral justification that is worthy of further exploration.[34] For the present we merely focus on the creative possibility of accepted rulings as having paradigmatic guidance within a moral practice.

To sum up, rulings may take various forms. They may be characterized in the first form as pure subsumptive judgments in applying existing rules in a moral practice to normal circumstances. In the second form, rulings are judgments which are interpretations of the rules to fit uncertain or problematic cases. In this form rules may be said to be modified, qualified, altered in their scope of applications. Again, the second form may be regarded as subsumptive in nature. Once the rules are qualified by exceptions, they retain their force and the ruling simply reformulates the rules so that particular situations may be viewed as instances within the scope of these moral rules. In the third form, which is the major emphasis of our discussion, rulings are judgments in abnormal or exigent situations that do not appear to be manageable within the given set of moral rules. These rulings are field dependent and situation dependent. For the moral agent, here is the domain of creativity in which moral pioneers preach and live their lives. The rulings, in this form, may inspire a following and may be accepted within a moral practice, as we have seen in the living influence of paradigmatic individuals in different moral practices. Many moral practices are dominated by these paradigmatic individuals; indeed, one way of referring to moral practices is by referring to these dominating and inspiring individuals. Thus we speak of Christian or Confucian moralities. For different moral agents living within these moralities, Jesus Christ and Confucius are the dominating focuses of their moral lives. These persons are the ones who invest their moral practices with a new character and function. But they do not preclude ordinary agents from becoming pioneers in their own way, in the exercise of rulings that may become paradigms for solutions to other persons' problematic situations.

F. Rulings and Respect for the Moral Practice

The preceding section stressed the justification of rulings in exigent circumstances in terms of reasonableness rather than the rationality of a moral practice. Our position is that of a reflective moral agent who focuses on both the field-dependent and situation-dependent character of his rulings. A question inevitably arises: How are these two features of rulings to be reconciled? In normal cases, the question on relevance of rules to particular situations does not arise. But in exigent situations where a ruling is made on, say, the irrelevance of a moral rule, the agent may appear to a fellow agent within a moral practice to be violating a rule. As moral agents we may learn from our moral practice that such rules as "Stealing is wrong," "Lying is wrong," and "Promises ought to be kept" have a *de jure* or authoritative force. How then can we account for an agent's acceptance of this authority and simultaneous disavowal of its relevance in rulings in exigent circumstances? One agent may feel justified in breaking a rule, offering reasonable explanation and description of his personal predicament. But it is a common experience among sincere moral agents to *feel regret* in making a ruling that contravenes the requirement of a given rule in the eyes of a fellow agent. Assuming that this is the case, how can we account for this feeling of regret in, say, breaking a promise in favor of an action which an agent deems to be especially called for in *his* exigent situation? In this discussion, we need to take the position of the judge in trying to understand the agent's rulings in exigent cases.

If we follow our first strategy discussed in Section 6C, we are likely to describe an action that justifiably breaks or violates a moral rule (henceforth a JB action) as an action that falls within the intended operative scope of a moral rule. Thus if an agent breaks his promise to another person, *A*, believing himself justified in doing so, his action is deemed justified insofar as he can produce a justification acceptable to *A* as an exception in some manner sanctioned by the rule "Promises ought to be kept." The agent's action, based on his ruling in an exigent situation, is then understood or described as a JB action, since it falls within the intended scope of the application of the moral rule. According to this common view, moral rules have implicit escape clauses that sanction such actions.

In contrast to this view, Urmson recently pointed out that "when we have an authoritative rule we must distinguish our making an exception to, or breaking, the rule from the rule itself admitting, perhaps even specifying exceptions."[35] Thus a JB action cannot be plausibly characterized as an instance of a class of recognized exceptions to a moral rule. From the fact that lying, promise breaking, and stealing can sometimes be justified, it does not follow that the rules in question have implicit exceptions. In understanding a JB action we should perhaps distinguish two different types of question: the question of applying and the question of breaking or making an exception to the rule.[36] The second question presupposes that a ruling or judgment or decision on the relevance of rules is already made. In problematic cases when an agent is uncertain of what he ought to do, he may be wondering whether certain moral rules *relevantly* solve his problems. If he decides on a JB action, say, breaking a promise, he has in effect made a ruling that the rule "Promises ought to be kept" is *irrelevant* to his present predicament. In accordance with this ruling, he feels justified in doing an act contrary to the requirement of the rule of promise keeping; he is not making an exception to the rule. From the point of view of the rule, his action is a JB action precisely because a fellow agent not involved in his predicament can describe it as an instance of violation of a relevant rule. But the point of view of the fellow agent does not necessarily coincide with the point of view of the agent who is reflecting upon the application of moral rules to *his own case*. Thus he may feel justified that in his own case, the fellow agent's point of view does not apply. From the agent's point of view, any application of moral rules presupposes a ruling on the relevance of rules to actual circumstances. The moral rules themselves do not contain criteria for application.

As Arthur Murphy reminds us, we learn our moral rules as reasons for acting. "When such reasons clearly apply, and where no counter reasons relevantly appear, a good man will see and do his duty without argument or question."[37] Thus in normal circumstances of our life, the authoritative rules we learn and accept constitute sufficient reasons for acting. In these normal situations, no special ruling is required since rules are obeyed without question. A common judgment on the relevance of moral rules is presupposed. In these normal situations, the fellow agent's point of view coincides with that of the agent. A discrepancy between the two points of view occurs in problematic cases confronted by the moral agent. If he decides on a JB action, he must have special reasons for doing so. One essential element in justification for a JB action appears to be a plea for a special circumstance. If an agent fails, say, to fulfill his promise, he must offer a reason to the promisee. Such a reason may involve a ruling on his part on the relevance of another rule which issues a requirement incompatible with that of the promise-keeping rule. He *must* have a reason for not keeping the promise. But such a justification need not be acceptable to the promisee. However, if the promisee agrees with his ruling in his own problematic case, he may be relieved of his obligation or postpone the fulfillment of his promise to some future date, depending on the nature of the promise.

Thus an action may be understood as a JB action when two conditions are satisfied: (1) the agent in question has a reason for not complying with a moral rule judged from the fellow agent's point of view as a rule that relevantly applies to his own case; and (2) the agent's action must be such that it can be plausibly described as an action performed in an abnormal or exigent circumstance, i.e., a situation that is not normally understood as an obvious case for the application of the rule. From condition 1, Urmson rightly points out that a JB action cannot be adequately characterized as a case of recognized exception of a relevant rule. In other words, a fellow agent's judgment on the relevance of a rule does not logically imply that a JB action is a recognized exception to a given rule, for the agent may deem the fellow agent's rule inapplicable to *this* case. The agent's reason for not complying with the rule, of course, can be independently assessed. Condition 2 points to the sort of assessment that is relevant to the agent's point of view. The circumstance must be such that it can be described as abnormal or *exigent*. The situation may be also described as an *exceptional* one, not in the sense that it is a recognized exception in our understanding of the function of rules, but in the sense that the situation is judged to be outside the scope of the application of a seemingly relevant rule. Acceptable justification depends on taking a *reasonable* rather than a rational attitude toward the moral practice. Reasonableness, as we have remarked, remains an open notion not amenable to a theoretical formulation.

The fact that a fellow agent's description of a JB action as contravening a moral rule is abstractly regarded as an appropriate description in part accounts for the agent's reluctance to make rulings against the application of a seemingly relevant rule. Again, Urmson justly remarks that a departure from the explicit injunction of an authoritative rule is "always hazardous and a matter for regret." "If John Doe breaks a trivial promise to Richard Roe with justification, he should still regret having broken it and an apology is due."[38] Thus for a concerned moral agent, a JB action is not to be taken lightly, since moral rules are considered to possess authoritative force. The regret that accompanies a JB action is a consequence of serious commitment to moral rules that are constitutive of a moral practice.

When an agent accepts a moral rule as his principle of conduct, his acceptance implies that he is to be bound by its injunction whenever it is judged relevant to actual situations. When he is placed in an exigent circumstance he may make a ruling on the irrelevance of a seemingly relevant rule. Although he may feel that a rule seems to have a relevant application, his ruling tells otherwise. His feeling of *regret* or of the need to make an apology or amends for, say, a broken promise is a consequence of the seriousness and sincerity of his commitment to the promise-keeping rule. Thus the rule, in the abstract, is always a relevant consideration. Such an abstract consideration has force or import for a concerned moral agent regardless of his special or exigent situation. As a consideration it does not logically dictate the outcome of the agent's deliberation and decision in exigent cases. When it drops out of account in the final verdict, it loses its applicability to his situation. But the force of the prior commitment to the function of moral rules remains unaffected. Thus the agent feels the need to apologize, make amends, and explain his conduct. His feeling of regret in performing a JB action is an expression of *respect* for the moral practice, but not a constitutive feature of his ruling or judgment of relevance.

If the foregoing remarks offer a sound explanation for the feeling of regret that accompanies a JB action, the justified breaking of a moral rule is compatible with the acceptance of moral rules as having a practical and authoritative force. Furthermore, a strict or rigorous construction of the function of moral rules appears to be compatible with a recognition of respect for their practical force even in an exigent circumstance that prompts the moral agent to rule them out as irrelevant. After all, as Kant rightly observes, respect for moral law is a consequence of our recognition of the force of a moral practice. It is a consequence of the commissive character of moral performances. The point may be brought out more clearly through a distinction between the *practical* and *actuating* force of moral rules. The practical force of moral rules lies in the agent's recognition of moral rules as relevant considerations in moral thinking and doing. But this recognition does not entail their actuating force in particular, concrete cases of deliberation. The actuating force of a moral rule depends on a ruling or judgment of relevance. It is the agent that actuates the practical function of moral rules. Respect for the practical force of a moral rule is thus compatible with its actual irrelevance in particular cases. Kant observes that respect is an effect of the moral agent's consciousness of the Moral Law and, consequently, an incentive to the practice of morality. But respect is not a constitutive feature of actions in the occurrent sense, nor of our judgments of the rightness or wrongness of action.[39]

The significance of the notion of respect for a moral practice lies in its relation to acts of moral acceptance, i.e., acceptance of moral rules as having practical and authoritative force. One's expression of sorrow or regret need not be a mere admission of a wrong deed, but a tribute to the obligatory character of the moral practice which one sincerely accepts (so also the feeling of righteous indignation at a wrong deed of another). However, the respect for a moral practice does not define the nature of moral feelings. What makes certain feelings peculiarly moral perhaps lies in the seriousness of our assent to the moral practice. In a more contemporary idiom, we may say that respect is noncontingently related to acts of moral acceptance. One cannot be said to accept or adopt a moral practice without a corresponding respect for it. A commitment without the respect for the practical force of the content of the commitment cannot be regarded as a serious one. One wonders whether it can be called a commitment at all.

We speak of "feelings of respect," but unlike moral feelings, which are context dependent, respect is a generic characteristic of moral acceptance. The feeling of respect may be said to be a qualitative feature of moral experience, not a cognitive one. To appreciate a JB action accompanied by the feeling of regret is to pay heed to this qualitative feature of our moral life.

G. Problems and Perplexities

The three forms of ruling do not exhaust the creative dimension of moral agency. They are discussed more in terms of the governing form and background of the moral life. Moral agents are persons also actuated by certain wants, purposes, ideals, and aspirations. Situations that appear perplexing and uncertain to an agent may concern him *alone* rather than as a member of a moral community. The question "What shall I be?" or "What is the meaning of my life?" may be one that is perplexing in being of a nonproblematic form. These questions may be viewed as *perplexity indicators* rather than *problem indicators*. This distinction is a distinction of two attitudes toward moral questions. When uncertain situations give rise to questions formulable in problematic forms, they are viewed as problems to be solved. A problem, if it is intelligible, points to some solution. Our discussion of rulings thus far focuses on uncertain situations as problem indicators. A moral agent may well assent to discussion but remain disturbed about certain questions that concern him as a person. He may be raising questions that are perplexity indicators rather than problematic ones. As philosophers we are more inclined to treat all perplexity indicators as problematic. In the case of perplexity indicators, it is the questioner who is perplexed. Asking a question may simply be a symptom, an indication of the questioner's state of mind. Questions as problem indicators are subject to rational or reasonable assessment. Questions as perplexity indicators, as Wittgenstein saw, call for treatment or therapy rather than problematic formulation. But therapy, to be effective, would need to yield an "insight" into the questioner himself—perhaps a sort of Socratic self-knowledge. Or it might take the more nebulous and elusive form of Zen enlightenment. In this way, questions may be answered without being problems that are solved.

The distinction proposed above is not offered as a contribution to the logic of questions. This distinction is important in understanding the different dimensions of the moral life. Questions of a reflective moral agent within a moral practice may take an ambiguous form. The question "What shall I be?" may be taken in the traditional sense of being a problem about the meaning of life, a problem calling for a solution in terms of an ideal norm or purpose that is worthy of pursuit. Traditional moral theories in part purport to answer the quest for life's meaning by offering solutions to the agent's question. The same question, on the other hand, may be interpreted as a perplexity indicator. The agent who asks the question may be perplexed over the significance of *his* existence even if he already possesses a certain policy or plan for his life. He may come to question the policy of life itself and actions that are measured in its terms. "What shall I be?" may be a question of "What sort of quality should my life have?" This may be called "a quest for a *style of life*" that satisfies a person's idiosyncratic craving. Unlike the answers in terms of ultimate end, perhaps the appropriate answer to a perplexity lies not in norms to guide conduct but in another notion of ideals as endowing quality to a life analogous to a literary or musical theme to be developed (Section 7E). The two interpretations of the question need not be incompatible. It all depends on the temperament and character of moral agents. The paradox, perhaps central in a man's moral life today, is this: in seeking for a style of life that is idiosyncratic and personally satisfying, the content and actions of the individual are subject to impersonal assessment. So long as we live a form of life, our conduct is ineluctably a topic of assessment by our fellow beings. Even if our personal striving in answering perplexities—our quest for styles of life—is of the utmost importance to us as individuals, our actions intrude on the public domain. They are items to be assessed rather than idiosyncratic marks of persons to be *appreciated.*

Rollo May remarks, "The striking thing about love and will in our own day is that, whereas in the past they were always held up as the *answer* to life's predicament, they have now themselves become the *problems.*"[40] A predicament may be said to be a situation that poses the perplexity indicators, the state that induces a man to wonder what he will be. Philosophies of Wisdom of the past may be construed as attempts to answer these predicaments by showing how these predicaments could be met and questions answered. In this sense they provided insights into the human predicament. No doubt with respect to the question on the meaning of life they often interpreted this question as a problem to which philosophical views are offered: competing views are assessed in terms of their power and adequacy as solutions to the problem. Moreover, insofar as they represent alternative solutions to a problem, the moral agent's inability to arrive at a rationally agreed upon solution would make these answers problematic. Dewey sees this point but appears to neglect the power of traditional philosophy in providing insights. The question is: What makes some of them insights into human situations? Certainly reflective moral agents are confronted in his milieu with a great variety of "pictures and images" of human life.[41] What makes one picture rather than another an answer to a predicament, providing an insightful way of looking at a predicament?

An insight into a predicament is an insightful answer to that predicament. Its nature lies in its ability to make itself relevant to that situation, whether that of a particular person or his cultural predicament. Insights that claim to be universal are justified in terms of the experience of recurrent predicaments. Philosophic insights are often justifiably claimed to be universal insights. However, changes in the human condition are bound to bring with them new predicaments and the corresponding need for new visions. The power of the old insights may thus become problematic when they are assented to without reflection upon their relevance to present situations. Their relevance may be relocated to give them life, or new insights may be needed. Philosophy, in reflecting upon the present moral predicament, can be a powerful instrument in generating new visions. Moral philosophy, in particular, can bring its own reflections to bear on the moral life, thus becoming a humane and human enterprise.

Moreover, insofar as a moral agent is in search of his own idiosyncratic identity or style of life, the insight sought is *more* a particular than a universal one. The question of the moral agent, as a perplexity indicator, remains primarily a personal one, for any insight in this sense is tied to a particular predicament as answer to a particular question. Mere statement of universal insights does not by itself establish their legitimacy and authority. Their authority has to be vindicated by the moral agent himself, the particular person whose predicament these insights answer.

In general we cannot classify the variety of perplexity indicators of moral agents, for these questions concern the questioners' own being as idiosyncratic persons. These perplexity indicators, being nonproblematic in nature, are not matters of external form of personal morality, but matters that concern every reflective person's interior life. Being nonproblematic, the questions are not intellectual questions that call for solutions. Here we are in the region of the "aesthetic" dimension of morality—a dimension that calls for understanding and appreciation rather than cognitive judgment.

To return to the question of relevance of rules to particular circumstances, we now should emphasize another sort of ruling, i.e., the judgment of relevance of rules and situations to a moral agent's quest for a style of life. His perplexity indicators may be elusive, but considerations of what may be termed *personal-valuational factors* may come into play in a person's rulings on the relevance of moral practice to his own life. We have attempted to point to this region that borders on the aesthetic dimension of morality. It remains a region to be explored. Moral rules may appear to be foreign to this region, but they remain the regulative conditions for personal strivings. Rulings, in personal valuational form, witness a greater diversity of morals. Perhaps many of our contemporary moral issues and perplexities arise from the intrusion of this sort of ruling. But before we attempt to adjudicate conflicting moral views that involve personal-valuational factors, we must first attempt to understand these factors. In the following chapter we move toward the region of personal idiosyncratic morality. In particular I attempt to elucidate the notion of styles of life and the ideals that have a role to play in a reflective moral agent's quest for a meaning in his life.

7

Dignity of Persons
and Styles of Life

Perhaps independent of the constitutive content of particular moral practices, to many reflective contemporary moral agents the notion of human dignity has a compelling normative force. The notion may be said to be an expression of moral principle that underlies our recurrent attitudes toward the disregard and contempt for human rights exemplified in racial discrimination, slavery, and the like. We may call such a principle, which is not tied to particular moral practices, a *transmoral principle,* and we may consider it a prime candidate for inclusion in a set of universal *moral principles* related to specific moral practices (see Section 5C). The notions of dignity, justice, and freedom appear to be such transmoral principles recognized by members of the United Nations. The Preamble of the Universal Declaration of Human Rights calls for "recognition of the inherent dignity and of the equal and inalienable rights of all members of the human family as the foundation of freedom, justice and peace in the world." If all reflective agents accept this *principle,* the concept of dignity may well be regarded as an expression of an intrinsic part of our contemporary form of life that bids us to regard men as persons rather than things.

Recent moral philosophers have justly devoted their attention to the importance of this normative concept of dignity as in some way indispensable to the analysis and elucidation of moral life. Much of the discussion appears under the title of "respect for persons." Some philosophers of law have also employed the concept in their legal theory.[1] The discussion is in part inspired by Kant's conception of moral agency, particularly the Principle of Humanity, which enjoins us "to treat humanity, whether in your own person or in that of another, always as an end and never as a means only."[2] Stock, for instance, states that "the right attitude to other persons within the scope of one's action is to treat them as persons, as existing in their own right, rather than as instruments of desire or as particular instances of a class (child, shop-keeper, servant, etc.)" and regards this attitude as the "sense of Kant's injunction to treat persons as ends in themselves, not merely as means."[3] This attitude also finds a forceful echo in the Continental philosophy of man, which stresses the uniqueness of man's decision, choice, and action. In this chapter we discuss a conception of dignity that is distinct yet related to the formal conception derived from Kant's moral philosophy. This notion of dignity, which we term a *performative* conception, is intimately connected with the notion of styles of life. I do not propose to analyze the concept of dignity, but rather to focus upon the *ideal* dimension of moral agency. This preliminary elucidation of the notion of styles of life I hope will be useful and illuminating in understanding one dimension of moral experience.

A. Formal and Performative Conceptions of Dignity

In Kant's moral philosophy, moral agents are regarded as *persons* rather than as *things* because they are essentially ends-in-themselves, and as such constitute an object of respect.[4] As an end-in-himself, a person possesses *dignity* rather than market or affective price. According to Kant, "Whatever has a price can be replaced by something else as its equivalent; . . . whatever is above all price, and therefore, admits of no equivalent, has a dignity."[5] The Principle of Humanity, as an expression of the moral law or the Categorical Imperative, embodies this distinction between persons and things. Ultimately dignity is a peculiar moral worth that persons possess not by virtue of any empirically describable property, but by virtue of the nature of the moral agent "who obeys no law except that which he himself gives." The idea of the dignity of persons thus ultimately rests on the autonomy of the will characteristic of rational agents in general. Kant's insight lies in unveiling the basic presupposition of moral agency in stressing a rational capacity of moral agents in the exercise of autonomy in the context of rule-governed behavior.

What I am calling the Formal Conception of Dignity is related to Kant's notion of moral agents as autonomous wills. However, I do not intend to ascribe this conception to Kant, but rather to suggest a view that could be developed from certain remarks of his, in order to form a basis for contrast with our *performative* conception of dignity. Kant remarked that "all respect for a person is only respect for the law [of righteousness, etc.] of which the person provides an example." The respect for the moral law is said to be "the consciousness of submission of the will to the law, combined with an inevitable constraint imposed by our reason on all inclinations." Further, "respect remains a tribute we cannot refuse to pay to merit whether we will or not; we can indeed outwardly withhold it, but we cannot help feeling it inwardly."[6] Taking these remarks together, they suggest what we term a Formal Conception of Dignity. The tribute to merit is a tribute paid to moral law rather than to persons as individuals entitled to respect on the ground of personal dignity. On this conception, the dignity of persons is an exemplification of the dignity of moral law. It is moral law that constitutes the ultimate ground of respect for persons. The dignity of persons is thus parasitic upon the person's capacity for rule recognition and rule obedience. Respect for persons amounts to respect for a common capacity of human beings to satisfy the obligatory requirements of a moral practice.

If we now consider this conception of dignity as the basis of Kant's Principle of Humanity, the notion of person which underlies the statement of the formula is a *formal* and *generic* notion, in the sense that it conceives of persons primarily in terms of their generic rather than idiosyncratic capacity.[7] Respect for persons is not an expression of regard for persons as unique bearers of proper names. On this conception, the moral rules that concern persons conceive of persons as abstract subjects for moral consideration rather than as concrete individuals possessing recognizable idiosyncratic characteristics. This conception of person underlies a main feature of the rule model of morality. Persons are morally significant insofar as they bear certain relation to their moral practice. They are not special objects of moral consideration within the context of a moral practice. A moral agent's acts are to be assessed in light of the rules, rather than as matters that exemplify idiosyncratic features to be appreciated. Our judgment of his actions is an *impersonal* judgment. The persons who are the subjects of our moral judgment could in principle remain anonymous, for the interest in judgment lies in the assessment of the acts rather than *personal* character. Judgments, in light of the constitutive content of a moral practice, thus do not require any special concern for persons as they are in themselves. The dignity one ascribes to persons appears to be a *borrowed* dignity. The person's merit remains derivative from that of the moral rules. In this way, the Principle of Humanity, as formula, is a formal expression of a moral notion. This principle expresses a formal rejection of certain types of rules and acts as morally permissible. The notion of dignity that underlies the principle does not by itself ascribe any intrinsic merit or worth to persons *qua* persons.

We may contrast this formal conception with a *performative* conception of dignity. This conception is in part implicit in our ordinary thinking. One ordinary definition of "dignity," though not the only one, focuses upon "the presence of poise and self-respect in one's deportment to a degree that inspires respect." This conception emphasizes the *characteristic manner* of performance. For me to respect someone in this sense, there must be something *distinctive* about him, some deed that I deem to be a worthy feature of his *being,* not merely an exemplification of a moral requirement within a moral practice. Respect for a person is a recognition of the person as one who possesses certain meritorious and idiosyncratic features. A person's deed is regarded as having a personal signature, so to speak, of a distinctive form. Dignity of person is an award given by others that expresses a recognition of personal merits as idiosyncratic achievements. This conception of dignity requires a person be a unique bearer of a proper name. Dignity and respect are feats of personal accomplishment rather than anonymous compliance with moral rules.

I suggest that the formal and performative conceptions of dignity are distinct but related. The one expresses a formal principle of a moral practice, the other a substantive principle of personal morality. The task remains to determine the connection between the two with a due recognition for the *de jure* character of a moral practice. We shall next attempt to carry out this task by way of a distinction between two points of view we adopt regarding moral agents in general.

B. Human and Technical Points of View

Modern society frequently is criticized for reducing man to a series of functions and roles. In the words of Marcel, "The individual tends to appear both to himself and to others as an agglomeration of functions. As a result of deep historical causes, which can as yet be understood only in part, he has been led to see himself more and more as a mere assemblage of functions, the hierarchical interrelation of which seems to him questionable or at least subject to conflicting interpretations."[8] The peculiar force of this critique of modern society lies in its insistence on the importance of the distinction between two not necessarily exclusive points of view about men. To adopt Williams' terms, this is the distinction between the *human* and *technical* points of view. "There certainly is a distinction, for instance, between regarding a man's life, actions or character from the aesthetic or technical point of view, and regarding them from the point of view which is concerned primarily with what it is *for him* to live that life and do those actions in that character."[9] From the technical point of view, a man's life is the playing of certain roles. His successes and failures *as* a man are judged in terms of role playing. Something seems to be left untouched in adopting this point of view—the individual *qua* individual as having certain sentiments, feelings, purposes, and aspirations. Here a man is regarded as an efficient or inefficient occupant of positions and roles in society. The rough or fine texture of his interior life is often deemed irrelevant from this point of view. The *human* point of view, on the other hand, views man as in some fashion independent of his roles. It requires us to see man from his own point of view, as the idiosyncratic possessor rather than as a mere assemblage of titles and roles.

Within the social and moral institution of life reflective moral agents do sometimes experience the tension between these apparently opposing points of view. In playing a particular role, I may be quite conscious that *I* am playing the role. As a teacher, for instance, I also feel that I am a human being who is playing the role. I am more than the various roles that I play throughout my life. The technical point of view sees me only from the position of an outsider. From this point of view I am an *open book* subject to technical criticism. My interior reservoir of intentions, desires, and purposes, not identical with role expectations, is assigned to the limbo of the meaningless. My opposition to the technical point of view and criticism of society is a demand that I be recognized for what I *am,* not for what I do in playing a particular role. The same sort of attitude may be adopted while one is engaged in moral practice as consisting of a body of rules and obligatory requirements. Here is the attitude that demands self-respect and respect for my privacy, not in order that I may conceal, but in order that I may be recognized for the peculiar privacy with a *style* of my own. When this attitude is generalized, it becomes a demand for recognizing the diversity of individual styles of life. This demand, of course, does not ascribe any content to these styles of life.

The root of this tension between the two points of view perhaps lies in our occasional experience of the radical disparity between what we ought *to do* (as required by social roles and moral rules) and what we want *to be* or what we think we ought to be. Perhaps the tension may be partially eased if we recognize the possibility of personal idiosyncratic contributions in playing the roles or in observing the requirements of moral rules. Here we may introduce a distinction between two different sorts of description of performance: *role performance* and *style of performance.*[10] As an example we may take the moral rule that governs promise keeping. Insofar as we understand and accept the rule that "promises ought to be kept," and in a particular situation of promise keeping, say, returning the money that I borrowed from another person, the moral rule does not by itself prescribe the *manner* of its fulfillment. My *manner* of fulfilling the promise does not form an essential part of the description of promise keeping. Assuming that promise keeping is the only relevant consideration, *how* I return the money (i.e., cheerfully, gratefully, courteously, indifferently, etc.) is in a sense irrelevant to my keeping the promise as long as I returned the money that I borrowed from another.

Thus an individual may bring certain personal qualities to bear in the performance of his roles without these qualities being prescribed by the content of the role performance. Insofar as we view the individual's actions as embracing the style of performance consisting of idiosyncratic features, we are to that extent focusing on the *quality* or the *texture* of the actions. Here we have, so to speak, the qualitative occurrence of *intrusive novelty,* in the sense that the personal features somewhat intrude themselves in the actions as describable in terms of role performance or as instances of application of moral rules.[11] These features can be accounted for in part in terms of the agent's character or personality traits. However, from the agent's point of view, the qualities exhibited may be viewed as satisfying various standards that are not necessarily tied to his moral practice. In an instructive essay, Horsburgh discusses a plurality of moral standards that are "concerned exclusively with our interior moral life and our reactions to the judgments which other moral agents may pass on our conduct, not at all with the judgments that we pass on the conduct of other agents."[12] Horsburgh calls our attention to three different sorts of standards:

1. *A self-respect standard* is a minimum standard a moral agent maintains—a standard "below which we cannot fall without the loss of self-respect." It is a standard of self-worth for maintaining a level of performance which varies from one agent to another. The application of this standard does not necessarily constitute a claim to merit or inspire respect from others in the performative sense. Though a per-

son can claim a recognition of personal integrity in terms of self-respect, his acting in accordance with this standard is an expression of his own expectations of what his actions should display. Where this action is regarded by others as meritorious, it can be awarded the title of dignity in the performative sense. However, other agents cannot reasonably deny the personal integrity of the moral agent in exhibiting idiosyncratic features not recognized by the moral practice. His style of performance may be appreciated as conformable to his standard of self-respect.

2. *An aspirational standard* is "a higher standard to which we aspire but more or less infrequently attain, a standard which arises out of that dissatisfaction with ourselves which issues in a desire to make moral progress." The aspirational standard sets a target for moral progress.[13]

3. *The inspirational standard* is "a standard of moral perfection by means of which we rank all other standards." Thus an inspirational standard may simply be an ideal *theme* in which one strives to develop and not solely a *norm* to measure one's conduct. We shall pursue this distinction later.

Seen in terms of the three different standards, admittedly varying from one moral agent to another, the style of performance need not be an arbitrary display of idiosyncratic dispositions, but may be conformable to personal requirements that constitute the person's *sense of value* perhaps not recognized as part of the constitutive content of a moral practice. Thus a moral agent's action may exhibit two distinctive senses of "a successful performance." From the agent's point of view, he may be performing his role or acting in accordance with a moral rule in light of various personal standards which he deems important. From the point of view of role description, his success is assessed in terms of his compliance with role expectations rather than style of performance. Of special importance is the inspirational standard that embeds itself in some moral agents' performance. A rule-complying action may be embedded in an ideal character. For instance, I may keep my promise not just because it complies with the moral rule that promises ought to be kept, but because I believe that in keeping my promise I am expressing my concern and love for another person as in some way constitutive of my ideal of a moral life. In this light my promise-keeping action is more than just an instance of rule-governed behavior; it is embedded with an ideal. Although the moral rule is sufficient, from the point of view of other agents, for a judgment of my action, it is an insufficient means of understanding what I do. To appreciate what I am doing in this instance is to see how moral rules that are accepted as my principles are embedded with moral ideals that go beyond the minimal requirements of the moral practice. In morality we do not merely deal with rule regulation or judgment, we also need to understand and appreciate what moral agents do in light of their ideal requirements.

In making these remarks I do not mean to deny that moral ideals and rules may conflict, and that this conflict is a source of great tragedy. How one conceives and resolves this sort of conflict in the last analysis depends on one's posture toward ideals and rules. There is no adequate a priori picture of moral conflict. However, commitment to a moral practice involves an acknowledgment of certain basic rules as having an authoritative force in the regulation of personal ideal pursuits. For these basic rules to be effectively enforced, cooperation among moral agents is essential. From this point of view, only the posture that views the pursuit of personal ideals as subject to a basic regulation within the cooperative scheme of human activities is deemed worthy of attention. Domination of one ideal over another belongs to the region of reasonable persuasion conducted within the domain regulated by moral rules. Inspirational standards conceived of in terms of ideal norms may have in this way a critical role to play within a moral practice. But their effective role appears to depend in part on consensus on the moral practice as being embedded with a common ideal. Thus ideals of common good or welfare can be seen to be an effective instrument in moral criticism of social and political institutions. But when ideal norms are advocated as public standards, they are subject to the governance of basic moral rules. Ideal norms are diverse and have to be recognized as such. But this recognition does not preclude them from being subjects of assessment in terms of basic moral rules. Moreover, when the moral agents conceive of their ideals not as norms for measuring conduct but as *themes* that endow their activities with a quality and a style, these ideals need not conflict for they function primarily as inspirational standards that do not pretend to claim to being universally prescriptive norms. We shall pursue this distinction between ideal norms and ideal themes later in this chapter.

To return to our focus on the style of performance, a proper appreciation of the idiosyncratic features of an agent's conduct requires that we adopt the human point of view. It would appear that from the moral point of view, the intrusive personal features are subject to moral praise and censure. If our preceding remarks are plausible, only those features that appear to be compatible with the function of moral rules are possible candidates for a distinctive laudatory personal style.

Our performative notion of dignity in part finds its home in individual *styles of performance.* For other agents, not all styles of performance have intrinsic dignity; only those that give the performance a personal and persuasive force cry out for recognition. Here is the domain of what Hume terms "personal merits"—a region of personal constellation of mental qualities. In this region is found "every attribute of the mind which renders a man an object either of esteem and affection or of hatred and contempt; every habit or sentiment or faculty which, if ascribed to any person, implies either praise or blame and may enter into any panegyric or satire of his character and manners."[14] We are here in the realm of idiosyncratic personal existence. Personal merits can be an integral part of performance from the point of view of the actor. If the notion of *style* is to be reserved as a laudatory epithet, we should perhaps distinguish it from the *manner* of performance. We can then say that only the distinctively laudatory manner forms the style of performance. The point may clarified by considering man not merely as a role player or moral performer but as an individual exhibiting idiosyncratic features that form his *style of performance.* His style of performance may in part be a portrayal of his *style of life.* If styles of life constitute one sense of the meaning of life for moral agents, compliance with certain basic moral rules appears to be the indispensable condition that defines the limits of moral agents' pursuits. To insist on the necessity of producing merit claims in our notion of dignity is to pay heed to the limiting conditions that are set forth by our moral rules.

If the mere emphasis on assessing human conduct from the technical point of view bespeaks a danger in seeing man as a mere assemblage of functional instruments, the Kantian Principle of Humanity is in part a corrective to this danger. However, we are also faced with an equally undesirable danger in overstressing the human at the expense of the technical point of view, i.e., there is a danger of regarding men as bearers of values regardless of their content. Here moral rules and those rules that are encapsulated in social roles are at least the minimum requirements regulatory of the individual pursuit of dignity and styles of life. The human point of view, if it is to be construed as distinct and opposed to the technical point of view, appears to be a partial view of the reality of life situations. Both together serve as complementary reminders of the danger of one-sided exaggeration.

To see them as two different, though not opposed, dimensions of assessment of human conduct is to give both points of view their legitimate areas of employment. Both are context dependent; their useful employment depends on the contexts and fields of discourse.

C. Relation between the Two Conceptions of Dignity

The performative notion of dignity concerns the human point of view, which recognizes the idiosyncratic rather than the generic characteristics of human existence. We have suggested that dignity lies within the domain of personal merits that may be said to be characteristic of the styles of performance that in part betray the individual styles of life. Dignity is an award based on personal merit. A person cannot in this sense certify his own dignity. He can present merit claims for recognition of dignity. Dignity is an esteem that we express in recognition of personal excellence by virtue of which a person *distinguishes* himself. It depends on other agents' appraisal. This sort of personal distinction is not a mere matter of eccentricity or originality in a manner of performance. To regard a performance as *eccentric* is to take note of its unconventional character, i.e., to regard the manner of performance as in some way deviating from our conventional expectations. Eccentric behavior is unconventional behavior. Although it may be subject to praise or censure, an eccentric behavior, from the descriptive point of view, remains a mere divergence from conventional expectations of behavior. A mere difference does not constitute a personal distinction. On the other hand, a person's performance may be deemed *original* or novel without being distinctive in the normative sense. Sometimes when we characterize a person's performance as "original" we are simply drawing the hearer's attention to a feature (or features) of performance that we deem worthy of attention without commenting directly on the manner of performance. The characterization is an emphasis or focus on a *unique* difference distinct from the usual manner of behavior. Moreover, this sort of comment is often coupled with a normative intent, i.e., as a preliminary step toward an award of dignity. Where the noted features of the manner of performance are taken as grounds for personal merits, the features are regarded as marks of personal distinction or dignity.[15]

Our performative notion of dignity is related to the formal notion in that the Principle of Humanity sets the regulative limit for the pursuit of this sort of excellence. Morally speaking, one cannot strive to achieve the dignity of a style of performance by treating others as mere instruments for personal triumph and achievement. From the point of view of the moral requirements in the Principle of Humanity, every person is responsible for his own style of performance and style of life. Thus the moral point of view has often been regarded as a court of appeal for adjudicating conflicts between individual interests and aspirations. For any moral agent who assents, this point of view, from its commissive aspect, acquires a personal dimension. From the agent's point of view as a person with certain wants, desires, and aspirations, the moral point of view may acquire a special force. Thus it recently was claimed that "a moral point of view is a view about how life as a whole is to be lived. It affects everything that we do, not merely what we do when faced with a moral problem."[16] This way of regarding the moral point of view reflects our assent to the moral point of view as a regulative ground for what we do. Moreover, for an agent who rejects the moral point of view there still remains a sense in which his performance is subject to assessment in terms of moral rules. A performance is an action that occurs within a public domain. Where it conflicts with the criteria for assessment that govern the items in the public domain, the performance is subject to judgment in terms of these criteria regardless of its personal idiosyncratic features. Where the styles of performance do not conflict with these criteria, they may be candidates for an award of dignity. In this sense the award of dignity requires a certain level of rule obedience as a precondition.

If the formal notion of dignity that underlies Kant's Principle of Humanity furnishes a ground for moral judgment of actions, the performative notion of dignity appears to provide a ground for judgment of desert. Paradoxically, the performative notion offers no moral criterion for the judgment of desert, at least in the sense of a criterion that has both a rational and prescriptive force for all agents within a moral practice. Hume and his predecessors tend to look at sentiment rather than *reason* as the ultimate ground for the assessment of personal merits. Styles of performance must, in some sense, be a form of personal achievement. Our grounds for awards for dignity appear to be tied to our feelings of admiration and awe for those persons who are paradigmatic exemplars of personal achievement. We are for the present inclined to the Humean view on the legitimacy and significance of our moral sentiments in the award of dignity based on personal merits.

D. Ways of Life, Styles of Life, and Moral Ideals

Toward the end of Section 7B it was suggested that styles of performance of individual moral agents may in part be a portrayal of individual styles of life. Style of life is a notion we used to focus on the ideal
dimension of moral creativity. This focal notion of style of life (henceforth SL) requires a further elucidation. In Section 1B the distinction
between way of life (henceforth WL) and SL in both individual and
cultural senses was noted. We used the notion of moral practice as
synonymous with cultural WL and reflected on the possibility of moral
creativity with respect to moral rules and particular circumstances in
Chapter 6. As for cultural SL, our discussion on Confucian *li* or propriety in Chapter 4 may be taken as an attempt at a discussion of its
significance within the setting of a moral practice. What will occupy us
now are matters that pertain to WL and SL in their individual rather
than cultural significance.

In Chapter 2 the focal notions of WL and SL were used in terms of
the distinction between the *content* and *quality* of WL. The notion of SL
is used to accentuate the qualitative features of an agent's life and
performance. An adequate elucidation of SL depends on an explication
of WL, for a quality of a WL depends in part upon the agent's conception of the nature of his WL. It is the WL that gives the material
content to the SL. Our use of SL is derived from the use of "style" in
aesthetic discourse. According to Meyer Schapiro, "By *style* is meant the
constant form—sometimes the constant elements, qualities and expressions—in the art of an individual or a group. The term is also applied
to the whole activity of an individual or society, as in speaking of a
'lifestyle' or the 'style of civilization.' "[17] We have taken this quasi-aesthetic notion in focusing upon the quality and expression of the stuff of
the WL. An individual SL is the qualitative form of his WL viewed in
some way by the agent as giving certain significance or meaning to his
life. In this sense, SL can be a target of moral achievement, for a
person can live a WL and yet feel dissatisfied with his WL as devoid of
a quality of excellence. His WL may be seen to have a *telos* in the sense
of having a life plan or constant policy of life that is dominated by an
ideal, and yet he may be in search of an ideal telos that will give a
quality of excellence to his WL. The telos of an SL is thus more than a
constant policy of action in accord with an ideal norm, but an ideal of
excellence which if realized will display a qualitative texture—an ideal
quality that will pervade a WL with a life plan. The notions of WL and

SL are telic concepts. The point to note is that one may have a WL without an SL, though one cannot have an SL without a WL.

We may elaborate the notion of SL further by briefly commenting on Alfred Adler's use of the notion of style of life in his Individual Psychology.[18] The use of SL here has close affinity with and is in part indebted to some of Adler's uses, although unlike Adler I do not use it as a psychological construct or a normative concept that is tied to a specific moral criterion. Adler uses the notion of SL in part as a focal notion to stress the uniqueness of the individual. It is his maxim that "everything can be something else as well. The uniqueness of the Individual cannot be expressed in a short formula, and general rules—even those laid down by Individual Psychology which I have created—should be nothing more than an aid to a preliminary illumination of a field of vision on which individual can be found or missed." Adler sees the uniqueness as a life plan that gives unity and meaning of life to an individual developed from childhood, as a "law of movement," a life pattern that reveals the individual's attitude toward his community or the three life problems—"the problems of communal life, of work, and of love."

Many of Adler's remarks on SL disclose his use as a telic and holistic concept. His psychology is based primarily on a telic thesis that "considers all the manifestations of the human soul as though they were directed toward a goal."[19] The goal is abstractly formulated as a goal of overcoming or superiority, but Adler always focuses on the diverse variety of uniqueness in individual cases. "The goal of superiority with each individual is personal and unique. It depends upon the meaning he gives to his life. This meaning is not a matter of words. It is built up in his style of life and runs through it like a strange melody of his own creation. In his style of life, he does not express his goal so that we can formulate it for all times. He expresses it vaguely, so that we must guess at it from the indications he gives." Adler insightfully remarked that "understanding a style of life is similar to understanding the work of a poet. A poet must use words; but his meaning is more than the mere words he uses. The greatest part of his meaning must be guessed at; we must read between the lines. So, too, with that profoundest and most intricate creation, an individual style of life. The psychologist must learn to read between the lines; he must learn the *art of appreciating* life-meanings."

The notion of SL in Adler is thus a focal notion that directs attention to the unique and idiosyncratic quality that is characteristic of a WL or life plan. An SL is in this way an idiosyncratic organization of styles of performance. The styles of performance can be an expression of an individual SL. Like the term "original" noted previously, the notion of uniqueness has at least two different uses. Apart from its normative use, we may use "unique" in a way that draws attention to a characteristic that deserves attention without commending or recommending it. A work of art can in this sense be unique without in any way being outstanding or distinctive in the normative sense. In saying that "this work or person is unique," I may be not merely reporting or describing a characteristic but drawing my attention to a feature of the person or work that I think deserves attention, though I need not specify the appropriate criteria for desert. Thus the expression is used to focus on a feature that does not seem to fit our conventional criteria for classification or criteria for evaluation. Likewise, when we talk of uniqueness of an SL, we are merely drawing attention to the idiosyncratic feature that is characteristic of the texture of a person's WL. This is neither to commend nor recommend, but simply a use of a certain notion to talk about the ideal dimension of moral creativity that does not properly fit the description in terms of the moral practice embedded with a body of moral rules. Depending on one's normative ethics, an SL can be assessed in terms of its moral criteria.

Although Adler uses the notion of SL principally as a focal notion to illuminate a "field of vision," his interest lies primarily in a sort of normative psychotherapy. To Adler, as we have noted, the individual SL is essentially a way of dealing with the three problems of life—communal life or social responsibility, work or occupation, love and marriage. His interest seems to lie in his treatment of pathological life styles presupposing a normative criterion of "social interest" or "social feeling." There is in his works a distinction between "true" and "mistaken" life styles. According to Adler, "The answer we give to these three questions [i.e., the three problems of life], by virtue of our style of life, is seen in our whole attitude towards them. Since they are very closely connected with one another—and indeed because all three require for their proper solution an adequate amount of social feeling, it is easy to understand that everyone's style of life is reflected more or less clearly in his attitude to all of them." Adler envisages an ideal world of social feeling—"an imagined state in which all the problems of life are solved and all our relations to the external world rightly adjusted." He admits that this is a "regulative ideal, a goal that gives us our direction."[20] "Mistaken" life styles are thus to be corrected in terms of a normative criterion of social feeling which presumably lies at the heart of Adlerian psychotherapy. Whether or not Adler's Individual Psychology is an adequate psychological theory is not our concern here. What is important to note is that he seems to shift from one sense of SL to another without laying down a proper conceptual bridge. Unlike Adler, we use the notion of SL as a focal notion on the ideal dimension of moral creativity without committing ourselves to any theory of moral ideals that constitute the goals of SLs. We aim at an understanding, an appreciation of the idiosyncratic moral strivings. We leave the question of evaluation an open question for reflective moral agents. We share Adler's emphasis on the need of "the art of appreciating life-meanings" that are embedded in SLs but without implying a commitment to his normative psychotherapy or ethics. In effect our use of the notion of SL is compatible with any normative or psychological theory. Moreover, it is a tribute to Adler to use the focal notion in the context of a psychological theory, thus contributing to an understanding of personality in works of psychotherapy.[21] Whether it is an adequate theory is a question that lies within the proper domain of psychology. We merely take note here of his insight in focusing upon the uniqueness of individual SLs. Many of his remarks, as we have noted, point beyond psychology. They can easily be adapted to our interest in understanding moral creativity.

We now resume our discussion of WL and SL of individual moral agents. I have suggested that the notion of WL is a life plan or a policy of life that is dominated by a telos that is regarded by the individual as an ideal norm to guide and measure his conduct. The notion of WL focuses on the coherence and integration of an individual moral life. Viewed in light of a moral practice, the commitive moral agent may be regarded as in part reconstituting the content of his moral practice. We do not claim that all moral agents are dominated by a singular life plan in any consciously conceived fashion, nor are all moral agents properly understood in terms of the unity of a life plan. But for some reflective moral agents, their moral dilemmas may in part be understood not so much as technical problems but as difficult questions that call for an answer in some ideal life plan that would be significantly definitive of what life ought to mean for them.[22] If one pays heed to the moral rules, one's telos or life plan may be regarded as a partial codification of moral rules in terms of their import to his life. And since his life is anchored on a form of life shared by other agents, his WL can be regarded as a partial specification or articulation of the form of life that forms the background of his moral community. A WL may thus be seen in terms of either a comprehensive telos or a plurality of policies lacking in any unitary telos. If an individual has a comprehensive telos, this need not be understood in the exclusive sense of happiness or perfection. But the ideal of happiness, or perfection however conceived, thus focuses on an ordered unity that is characteristic of some individual life plans. In this way a comprehensive policy of life may be viewed in terms of happiness or perfection that characterizes some traditional ethical theories. Paton thus defines "a policy of life" as "a search for a man's happiness; it aims at a satisfaction of his individual desires; and such things as welfare of others are sought primarily as means to this. A life of this kind may be intelligent or prudent and even within limits wise: it is a life lived according to a universal rule, or perhaps better, a system of rules which we conceive for ourselves and according to which we will our actions."[23] But individuals have divergent conceptions of happiness. It is this divergence that characterizes ways of life. We thus prefer the notion of SL as a focal term to stress the diversities of individual life plans. A policy of life may also be taken in a noncomprehensive sense as a cognitive way of describing an individual dominating telos for particular problematic situations. In this sense various individuals may have radically different policies in dealing with the variety of life situations. Arthur Miller's refusal in 1957 to identify some writers as communists in the House Committee on Un-American Activities hearings may serve as an example.[24] Miller appeals to his "sense of being myself." This refusal resulted in a conviction for contempt of Congress. His policy not to inform on other writers *may* be derived from a comprehensive telos. But in context, it appears to be a policy of life directed to a particular situation. It is doubtful that he intends his appeal to be a universal rule in the sense that he advocates it to be a moral rule that governs all his actions, and those of other agents. Perhaps his act is a *way of being* that finds its expression in certain sorts of action. This expression need not be taken as a universal or dominant telos throughout his life. We would suspect that even if a moral agent has a telos that dominates his life at a certain period, he may change his telos from one period of life to another. Goals of WLs may in this way have strength and relevance relative to these periods of life rather than comprehensive life plans that remain unchanged throughout the lives of moral agents.

Few moral agents in my experience display single and dominating life plans. If a comprehensive life plan is an ordered unity or organiza-

tion of separate policies, the individual may neither have nor attain it. Moreover, a moral agent, though devoid of a life plan that can be specified in terms of a plurality of policies, may have an ideal telos in the sense of an ideal theme to be developed rather than a norm to assess and guide his moral activities—an ideal that *qualifies* or gives quality to his activities, an ideal telos of his SL. Thus his style of orientation to his moral practice, as we have seen in the case of paradigmatic individuals, can be understood as a way of endowing an ideal character to his moral practice without in any way advocating a new norm to replace the interpersonal significance of his moral practice. Moral ideals as *themes* to be developed by individuals may in this way characterize the SL, or individual "sense of being a person," of moral agents. From the standpoint of an individual SL, much of the agent's moral practice can be regarded as lacking import or adding no meaning to his life. A moral practice in this sense does not define the nature of individual ultimate concern or commitment. When an individual is faced with a moral dilemma, this situation may incline him to search for a style of life that he deems to be ultimately desirable and satisfying, that gives his life a meaning apart from compliance with the moral practice.

We must thus observe that the SL and WL of an individual are distinct but intimately connected. We can hardly speak intelligently of a quality of excellence or telos of an SL, except perhaps in an abstract way, without the stuff that is *qualified* or the strands that make up the quality. Policies of life, whether ordered in a unity or remaining a random plurality, compose the stuff or substance and endow it with a certain quality. A person in quest of a WL may in effect be exploring ways of living. His use of moral arguments, as Hare points out, may take the form of what he can accept as relevant to his life. "What we are doing in moral reasoning is to look for moral judgments and moral principles which, when we have considered their logical consequences and the facts of the case, we can still accept."[25] But we need to focus on "the sense of being a person" as a crucial determinant in this piece of exploration. An individual's exploration need not take the form of moral reasoning that is an adequate subject of a logical characterization. It may simply be a personal and idiosyncratic exploration that pretends to no claim to universalizability and prescriptivity. What one reflectively accepts as a telos of his way of life does not imply acceptability to everyone. Acceptance of an ideal, consequent upon reflective exploration, may remain a personal matter.

Implicit in our distinction between an SL and a WL is a distinction between two interpretations of the nature of moral ideals. A moral ideal may be taken in the normative sense of being a norm or standard of excellence conceived of by an individual as a telos of his WL. We call this an *ideal norm.* On the other hand, a moral ideal may be taken in a thematic sense of being an excellent quality that an individual wants to develop as a telos of his SL quite apart from the specific nature of his life plan or policies of life. We have called this an *ideal theme,* suggesting the diversity of idiosyncratic achievements that are not amenable to fixed rules of understanding. Thus our notion of SL focuses on the uniqueness of moral achievement that lies at the heart of our performative notion of dignity. In the sense of being ideal themes, actions in accordance with moral ideals give the definitive content to the ideals. Chapter 8 presents a more detailed discussion of the two interpretations of moral ideals. We may take note here that to an agent in quest of an ideal SL, the natural world may appear as "the place of all possible themes and styles. It is indissolubly an unmatched individual and a significance."[26]

William James reminds us that morality in the broad sense is an experiment in living:

> "Rules are made for men, not men for rules"—that one sentence is enough to immortalize Green's *Prolegomena to Ethics.* And although a man always risks much when he breaks away from established rules and strives to realize a larger ideal whole than they permit, yet the philosopher must allow that it is at all times open to anyone to make the *experiment,* provided he fear not to stake his life and character upon the throw. The pinch is always here. Pent in under every system of moral rules are innumerable persons whom it weighs upon, and goods which it represses; and these are the rumbling and grumbling in the background, ready for any issue by which they may get free.[27]

It was suggested earlier that rulings in exigent situations may be regarded as "experiments in paradigmity" for oneself and others. Rulings in terms of moral ideals may be regarded as experiments in the standards of inspiration. What one can accept in the ideal sense from his moral practice may be guided by an ideal telos that concerns what one's life ought to be. If these ideals are viewed as universal, they form the topic for individual experiments rather than prescriptions for all SLs and WLs. At the end the individual has to make his "decision of moral ideal" that gives meaning or significance to life as he lives it. It is a personal task and a personal problem. Moral theory and practice cannot provide a priori valid ideals without being subject to these individual experiments. In the case of rulings tied to a moral practice and particular exigent circumstance, the ruling when accepted by others as a paradigmatic guide to action can acquire a universal dimension. But this sort of universality is a consequence of acceptance by others as a paradigm, not an intrinsic feature of the original ruling. Likewise, when an experiment in moral ideals is deemed successful by other agents it can function as a universal standard of inspiration. The universality would be a consequence of public acceptance, not an intrinsic feature of moral ideals as ends of individual SLs and WLs.

What emerges from our inquiry into WL and SL are two senses of moral ideals, i.e., ideal norms and ideal themes. Traditional normative ethics attempts to provide us ideal norms rather than themes. In Aristotle, Aquinas, and utilitarian theories, moral agents are provided with ideal norms as life plans which resemble various sketches to be filled out. Thus the Contemplative Life, Life of Blessedness, or the Greatest Happiness may be proposed as the ultimate end of human life. Each is intended as a normative standard which individual moral agents are to approximate or realize regardless of their moral dilemmas or what they think they ought to be. These traditional moral ideals, however, may be taken by the individuals as ideal themes. The question of the meaning of life may be taken in either one of these senses, depending on whether it be regarded as a perplexity indicator or problem indicator, as these were distinguished in Chapter 6. An ideal theme sets the tone, so to speak, for its development without prescribing its content or the steps toward its realization. Any development by an individual is an accomplished quality. Degrees of achievement are possible with SLs. An accomplished development is thus an achievement of a concrete SL, a quality rather than conformity with a norm. The moral ideal of love or humanity may be taken, for example, as an ideal of love or norm of love.[28] As an ideal norm, love presumably can be understood quite apart from the actions and efforts of the individuals committed to it. As an ideal norm, it functions as a measure of actions before their concrete occurrence. It can function as a standard for ranking or rating conduct. Traditional moral ideals in normative ethics aim at establishing this sort of norm. When love, on the other hand, is taken in the sense of an ideal theme as a love for humanity, here it does not function as a normative measure. To develop the theme, say, by loving another person, is to endow our actions toward that person with a quality or style of concern. The theme of love as an ideal telos of one's

SL is one that pervades one's actions throughout one's life. A developed theme is thus a "consequential" or "resultant" quality of acts. The acts themselves, from the standpoint of moral practice, are of course subject to appraisal in terms of the moral rules. But an accomplished ideal theme cannot be reduced to a mere collection of assessible items. Being a moral person is in part having this developed theme.

In this discussion we have used the notion of theme as distinct from norm primarily in analogy with two uses of "theme" found in ordinary discourse. A theme may be "a topic of discourse or discussion" that allows a diversity of expressions of individual beliefs or opinions on the topic. So also a theme, as characteristic of musical composition, is a "melody forming the basis for variations or other developments in a composition." A theme thus allows for radically idiosyncratic developments that are not necessarily incompatible from a common standpoint. But in itself, a musical theme does not normatively prescribe how it should develop or determine the sorts of content that properly come within its meaning. The sorts of content depend on the creativity of individual artists rather than the compliance with generally recognized standards. So also in morality, personal styles of life cannot be reduced to combinations of generally recommended virtues or obedience to universally binding rules.

E. Style of Life as a Prospective Task

The styles of performance of a person at home with his cultural milieu may be deemed sufficient for that person's *sense* of being a person or idiosyncratic individual. Dignity in the performative sense does not pose a personal problem. Rules of civility and etiquette and other conventional manners of behavior suffice for constituting his style of life. But for persons dissatisfied with the conventional styles of performance, the quest for dignity becomes a quest for a style of life. It appears to be a quest for individuality or personal identity. Insofar as moral rules embedded in moral practice constitute the regulative condition for any performance, the quest for a style of life remains a task for personal accomplishment. Here we are confronted with a diversity of individual quests for styles of life—a domain of the "diverse, certainly incompatible and possibly practically conflicting ideal images or pictures of a human life, or of human life; and it is a region in which many such incompatible pictures may secure at least the imaginative, though doubtless not often the practical, allegiance of a single person."²⁹ The quest for a style of life is a quest for self-identity. The formal notion of dignity defines the morally permissible limit for the pursuit of a person's ideals or projects for personal accomplishment. It defines the morally permissible limit, in the sense that the adoption of the moral point of view constrains one to regard other persons' ideals and ends as having equal claim to realization. Insofar as our actions in accordance with the search for a style of life conform to the regulative requirement, we achieve some degree of personal dignity. Our actions will carry a personal stamp. What distinguishes this class of actions as *personal* is not the truistic point that they are done by persons, but rather done by persons in some idiosyncratic way. This is the region of first-personal characteristics. A person's *name* is thus essential to the award of dignity.

Here I think the common practice of Chinese in *naming* their children provides an instructive example. Among the educated Chinese families that I know of, before a child is born, a great deal of time is spent in the discussion and selection of a personal name that has a distinct evaluative meaning. This naming activity is regarded as important in that it provides an occasion for the parents or elders to express their wish of what the child should grow up to be. It sets a task for the child's future accomplishment. The selection of a name reflects the parents' ideal of what the child will be. The personal name is thus an embodiment of an ideal. Here the child is regarded, so to speak, as a task for accomplishment. The rub here, of course, lies in taking this activity too seriously. For if the naming activity is taken seriously by the child himself when he grows up, his name can become an agonizing burden. But we learn something from this practice of naming. The practice points to the notion of dignity as an award. A name, in this sense, is a promise for an award—a promissory note. We may observe here that if the person does not live up to his name, he is not punished for his failure, although the parents may express disappointment. If a person, on the other hand, in fact lives up to his name, he achieves an idiosyncratic distinction. And if his performance satisfies the regulative moral condition, as it is expected to, he may be called a *man of dignity*. In this naming practice, we find an elucidation of the notion of dignity as an idiosyncratic achievement.

If the style of life is regarded by the moral agent as a prospective task, the style of performance is something that can be accomplished in individual actions. The style of performance may indicate a rhythmic pattern of a person's character. Insofar as this rhythmic pattern serves as an organizing principle of personal qualities or merits, the style of performance may be viewed as a partial achievement of a style of life. A style of life, on the other hand, may be a conscious, reflective, and idiosyncratic organization of the styles of performance or of the diverse items of actions. It is thus to be distinguished from a mere pattern of regularity which bespeaks the point of view of the external observer. A mere pattern of regularity is only a possibility for a style of life; it is a necessary but not sufficient condition for having a style of life.

A style of life may be viewed as an organization of personal merits. For many reflective persons, it is a prospective task, for a man's achievement here is always uncertain. The future to be determined by one's actions is an open future. Life seems to call for a variety of appropriate merits in different situations. I may not be satisfied with what I am. What I think I ought to *be* is an ideal. There are degrees of dignity, since there are degrees of achievement of the styles of life. Here we have the radical disparity between the actual and the ideal. One may not be as one ought to be. Even a man who is said to have a style of life cannot himself lay claim to any distinctiveness that ought to be the object of universal respect. One sometimes experiences a sense of moral failure, a sense of guilt. No self-conscious individual can always be satisfied with what he is. Even if he has accomplished much that is idiosyncratically and socially important, there seems to be much that is left undone. The quest for a style of life is a personal moral predicament. It may depict the anguish of a moral agent in search of a *soul*—a distinctive moral identity that justifies fully his being a moral person. It is said that "our morality is formed of principles and ideals which we do not succeed in persuading ourselves to fulfill."[30] If this is so, it is because we seek a justification for our moral failure. This justification is a rationalization of our existence. This sort of reason gives us strength and will to lead a moral life. It may also be an excuse for failure and an excuse for not trying in despair of the possibility of success. The belief in God has at least this practical function for some moral agents. The belief appears to preserve the strength of these agents in the search for a *moral soul*—a style of life. It is this style of life that appears to *inform* the body of moral rules which one accepts as principles of conduct.

Dignity is an award for the idiosyncratic achievement of a style of life. The rule-obedience model of moral agency defines the legitimate scope and character of moral actions. In this model, actions may be viewed as *retrospective* in that they resemble the determinate character of past deeds. However, from the prospective point of view of a style of life, actions are the determining items that fall within the regulative scope of moral rules. What I think I ought to do, in terms of what I think I ought to be as a person with unique requirements of my own, does not depend on moral principles and rules, but on the ideal of what I ought to be. The burden of my actions lies in the future and not in the past. In the case of ideal themes, the present is a step in defining the distinctive content of the future. Here the moral agent as an actor looks to the moral judge in terms of principles and rules for their regulating possibility, but determines, in effect, the content and form of this possibility. As a moral actor, his action is a determination of an open future, not by way of the past, but by way of the prospective ideal of a style of life. Without some degree of realization, a mere contemplated style of life remains an abstract theme to be developed rather than a concrete form of the moral life.

The notion of human dignity is an evaluative notion. If what is discussed in the preceding sections has a point of convergence, it is a focus on two aspects of morality in the broad sense. The two conceptions of dignity point to two facets of the moral point of view: (1) as a court for adjudicating conflicts of interest and the diversity of individual strife for styles of life; and (2) as a demand from the human point of view for conditions that provide for the realization of styles of life as idiosyncratic achievements. The two conceptions of dignity thus have implications for the conception of an ideal society. Negatively, an ideal society that accepts dignity as its basic goal has as its main task the setting forth of limiting conditions for freedom in the pursuit of styles of life. Positively, depending on the resource and initiative of the moral members of the community, it has its task in promoting conditions for the realization of styles of life. These two sets of conditions may be termed conditions of *restraint* and conditions of *achievement*. Criticism of technological society from the *human* point of view is in part an insistence that technological advancement should be channeled toward the recognition of idiosyncratic strivings and aspirations. Here Kant's ideal of a "kingdom of ends" has real persuasive force, for there is a reciprocal regard and consideration among members of this kingdom engaged in autonomous legislation. But the conception of moral agency remains a generic one. In order to give recognition to the idiosyncratic character of moral agents, we need a conception of society governed perhaps by the ideal of *agape*—an ideal of a community of concern and sympathetic consideration, and an active promotion of the diversity of the individual styles of life.[31]

To pay homage to this ideal of *agape,* however, is not to suggest a panacea for all social ills. From the point of view of human dignity, the homage must be a real and active one, not simply a verbal pronouncement of its importance, but an active effort at instituting provisions for the elimination of unjust treatment of persons because of creed, color, race, and sex as well as provisions for creating conditions that make possible the realization of individual styles of life without conflict. These remarks are less an articulation of a conception of an ideal society than a reflection on human dignity and its consequence for any conception of an ideal society. From our study of the notion of dignity, we learn that though human beings have no price equivalent, they do have idiosyncratic values and merits. The formal conception of dignity urges us not to degrade humanity in its generic form; the performative notion urges us to promote the idiosyncratic achievements of humanity.

F. Styles of Life as a Dimension of Morality

In the realm of styles of life, we are not necessarily confronted with a substantive moral diversity, but a diversity of "pictures" or images of men termed by Strawson "the region of the ethical."[32] The question of "what I want to be" may in part be a question of the idiosyncratic arrangement of items in the life of a moral agent. Just as two beliefs that have the same factual content may be accompanied by different pictures, two different persons may have the same set of facts and yet arrange them quite differently.[33] Thus the lives of two persons may be constituted by the same set of acts, insofar as these acts are subject to public assessment, and yet in their performance they may exhibit two contrasting styles. The diversity of styles of life may simply be a diversity of idiosyncratic arrangements of items that are subject to public and impersonal assessment.

Because of the diversity of the pictures of styles of life, most contemporary moral philosophers have thought it wise to restrict the conception of morality to the study of the analytic component of the moral life, for this restriction enables us to focus on morality as a body of rules that somewhat lays bare the nature of the publicly assessible acts. The conception of moral agency remains a generic one. If the study of the logic of moral rules constitutes the cognitive *sense* of morality, we should not forget that from the point of view of moral agents, there is in the moral life also a region of responsive *sensibility*. To restrict our concept of morality to the aspect of rule-governed behavior appears to be arbitrary. The restrictive conception of morality tends to view man in terms of a rule-obedience model. Very much seems to be left out in man's morality: the "moral attitudes which emphasize the inexhaustible detail of the world, the endlessness of the task of understanding, the importance of not assuming that one has got individuals and situations 'taped,' the connection of knowledge with love and of spiritual insight with apprehension."[34] However, the recent plea to supplant the rule model by the "model of the painter" to emphasize personal moral creativity appears also to be quite one-sided. If the Kantian conception, as it is reflected in the rule model, limits itself to the publicly assessible zone of personal conduct, the alternative model of the painter points to the zone of personal vision. But the zone of personal vision and of styles of life does not speak with a single voice; it has no universal prescriptive force and authority. As an emphasis on a dimension of moral life, the new model justly counteracts our tendency to regard moral agents as merely satisfying a common way of life. But, at the end, to see the moral life in its various dimensions may require complementary rather than exclusive models of human experience.

Whether or not we accept the realm of styles of life as part of our concept of morality, we cannot deny that our judgment of personal merits of a style of life betrays our own *sensibility*. Judgment of another person is often tenuous, for it requires great effort at a sympathetic understanding and knowledge of the person. Admittedly our judgment here borders on the region of the aesthetic—a region of human experience that calls for *understanding* and *appreciation,* rather than impersonal and objective judgment.[35] Styles of life appear to be irreducibly and existentially discrete. From the qualitative point of view, two personal histories are not existentially parallel series. One may only hope to achieve an *appreciation* of the style of life through understanding. One's appreciation of another person's style of life need not be exclusively cognitive or emotive, for a style of life is more like a work of art. And as Goodman recently pointed out, "The work of art is apprehended through the feelings as well as through the senses. Emotional numbness disables here as definitely if not as completely as blindness or deafness. Nor are the feelings used exclusively for exploring the emotional content of a work. To some extent, we may feel how a painting looks as we may see how it feels."[36] Can we not construe personal styles of life as works of art in Goodman's sense? To appreciate them is not merely to feel but also to see the personal idiosyncratic features that emerge from their conduct. Our world, according to Finlay, may be seen as "an assemblage of contrasting privacies converging upon the common zone of publicity. The apartness of people's interior states does not, however, preclude basic similarity and analogy."[37] But what governs our judgment of the public zone should not blind us to the importance of recognizing the idiosyncratic display of the quests for achievement of styles of life.

8

Two Interpretations of Moral Ideals

A. A General Characterization

In Section 7E ideal norms and ideal themes were considered as two interpretations of moral ideals. The task of Chapter 8 is a further elucidation of the distinction between the two. As a preliminary step we offer a general characterization of the notion of ideal as a context for our discussion of the distinction without claiming to present a philosophy of moral ideals.

In pursuing our task we shall follow the lead of William James. According to James, "An ideal ... must be something intellectually conceived, something of which we are not unconscious, if we have it; and it must carry with it that sort of outlook, uplift, and brightness that go with all our intellectual facts." Further, "There must be *novelty* in an ideal—a novelty at least for him whom the ideal grasps. Sodden routine is incompatible with ideality, although what is sodden routine for one person may be ideal novelty for another. This shows that there is nothing absolutely ideal: ideals are relative to the lives that entertain them." And for an ideal not to remain a mere private object of intellectual possession or entertainment, it must have a certain *depth* that owes to "the dimension of active will."[1]

These remarks suggest three aspects of moral ideals. In its *cognitive* aspect, a moral ideal is essentially an idea, an intellectual vision or conception of an excellent type of experience or state of affairs deemed by a person as a desirable telos or target for his life's activities. The idea must appeal to the agent as a novel pursuit, as in some manner charming and attractive in offering a new light upon his life. But in order not to remain a mere abstract conception, a moral ideal (whether it be benevolence, love, happiness, or justice) must be viewed by the agent as having an actuating or transforming significance in his own life. We must thus take note of its *conative* aspect, the aspect in which a commitive agent enlivens his ideal with an active will to its realization. An agent's ideal must thus have a directive force. The intellectual vision is a vision of a standard for the assessment and orientation of the agent's way of life. An ideal also has an *affective* aspect: the conception of an intellectual vision brings with it a certain joy, a feeling of uplift and satisfaction in anticipating achievement. And when an agent concretely achieves his vision, his activities may terminate in a consummatory experience of ease and tranquility.[2]

Since our interest lies in the contrast between ideal norms and ideal themes, this discussion concentrates on their cognitive rather than conative and affective aspects. From the cognitive point of view, an ideal is an intellectual conception of an excellent state of affairs or experience to which a commitive agent owes his allegiance and guidance. As a telos or target of his activities, it is essentially prospective in character. The telos may be seen as a principle of organizing an agent's life's activities and as a "principle of selection and control . . . [i.e.,] the control of attention and selection of possibilities for approval."[3] Brightman points out that an ideal is not an empirical generalization, for it is a vision which an agent conceives and endorses, although an agent may come to commit himself to an ideal after a careful reflection and assessment of his past experiences. Perhaps an ideal may also arise prereflectively, "through an apprehension of absense, a lack of fulfillment, and a paucity of my being." The prospective nature of an ideal may arouse hope in an agent, as well as "moods of sadness, longing, despair, and guilt."[4]

To understand morality it is important to focus upon the nature of ideal vision as an inspirational standard, as a standard of moral excellence that may be employed by a commitive agent as having an impact upon his life. The distinction between ideal norms and ideal themes is offered as a way of viewing the transforming significance of ideal commitments. When an ideal, as a standard of moral excellence, is regarded by the agent as a *norm,* the agent would attempt to view his ideal as admitting of programmatic articulation. An agent may work out his vision in terms of one or many programmatic tasks that conform to his ideal. His vision may serve as a sketch, so to speak, for which blueprints may be constructed for concrete realization. The ideal functions as a norm of measure to assess actual conduct in the degree of approximation to the requirements set forth in his vision. A moral agent may view his ideal norm as having a personal or social import. In the personal sense, he may regard his ideal norm as applicable to his conduct alone. His ideal norm would thus constitute a telos for his way of life. An agent, on the other hand, may regard his ideal norm as having a nonpersonal or public significance. Ideal justice and benevolence, for example, frequently are viewed as ideals that concern all moral agents regardless of their personal significance. So construed, ideal norms are espoused as public and universal standards for judging moral rules and conduct. Ideal norms in the social sense may thus take on an *ideological* character which moral agents attempt to promote without regard to other agents' interests and personal ideal concerns, as the Nazis did during World War II.[5] Brightman observes, "This is indeed a tragic aspect of life, for ideals are principles of unity and organization, and yet they work toward diversity and disorganization . . . that there are ideals is much more certain than what they are or ought to be; and that they conflict with each other is as certain as they are."[6] Furthermore, in the social sense, ideals may conflict with rules embedded in one's moral practice. Where this is the case, it appears that certain basic moral rules have a prior claim for being regulative conditions for ideal pursuits. An agent of course may not acknowledge this priority of moral rules. But one can always point out to him the necessity of finding at least some rules, even if only procedural in nature, for regulating ideal pursuits. Certitude in the authority of one's ideal norm is always open to challenge and one needs to appeal to the necessity of discourse conducted within the domain of acknowledged public rules. And when our ideal norms play a key role in our attempt to cope with exigent situations, as reasonable agents, we need to engage in discursive vindication of our rulings in the face of challenge offered by fellow agents. This is not to suggest that social ideal norms of moral agents have no critical role to play with respect to a moral practice. Where more agents share the same ideal norm and view it as a standard for assessing actions within the domain of moral practice, this ideal norm can have a powerful influence in the shaping of actual conduct.

Taken in a personal sense, an ideal norm of one agent need not conflict with that of another, although it may conflict with a moral practice in particular problematic situations. What is an ideal norm for an agent makes sense only against the background of what he regards as important in his life. His ideal norm may be regarded as a personal standard for sketching an excellent way of life within a common setting in which other agents have their own visions of the good life. Where these ideals conflict with the moral rules in particular cases, basic moral rules have again a certain priority of claim to compliance. But in this region of diversity, we cannot set forth a superordinate method that settles all conflict of this nature. Again, we fall back upon reasonable persuasion if we are not to face the tragedy of conflict. So long as we regard ourselves as members of a moral community, we need to pay heed to our moral practice, even in particular cases when we feel compelled to depart from its obligatory requirements. We need to offer to other agents our ideal reasons and open them up to reasonable discussion without dogmatically assuming an ideological posture. Some moral agents' experiences of remorse in departure from moral rules with no repudiation of actions that led to the departures provide an understanding of their difficult moral predicament. As Phillips and Mounce remind us, "Moral insight into the possibility of remorse without repudiation may go hand in hand with other insights. It helps one to understand how people can feel an obligation to help others, and show compassion and pity, whether questions of rights are involved or not. These moral insights are connected with seeing that very often there is no clear choice between good and evil. Striving for decency does involve one in evil, but its purpose is to lessen the evil." We can hope only to understand personal ideal concerns rather than propose a general method for resolving conflict between ideals and moral rules. The rules have different import to different agents. And in the context of personal ideal norms, the import of these rules ultimately lies in their place within a personal scheme of values or way of life. Even if agents share the same moral principles, on particular occasions they may arrive at different decisions because of their different ideal norms. "The difference between such decisions is not likely to be resolved by argument."[7]

Before we turn to an ideal theme, note that an agent may not have a single ideal norm as a dominating or permanent telos in his way of life. As seen in Section 7D, he may have a plurality of policies of life without subsuming these policies under a scheme of values governed by a singular norm. However, each telos of a policy of life must still function as an organizing principle with respect to relevant types of situations. What I would like to stress is the possibility of an agent adopting a nonideological posture toward this plurality of policies. Thus he may adopt an *egalitarian* posture toward various ideal types of conduct, regarding these types as exemplifying a distinctive set of ends without a superordinate standard of unity. This contrasts with an *organismic* posture in which an agent espouses his ideal norm as an inclusive telos for assigning his interests in some sort of value scale. The organismic posture rests on a comprehensive and inclusive telos in which all activities are given a proper place within a value scheme.

Typically, self-realization ethics concerns the organismic posture in its stress on integration of capacities and dispositions of moral agents.[8] The pragmatists seem to stress the egalitarian posture in Dewey's doctrine, for instance, of the continuity of means and ends.

A different interpretation of moral ideals lies in conceiving the ideals as *themes.* Unlike an ideal norm, which is a telos of a way of life, an ideal theme is a conception of a quality of life that forms the telos of a style of life. An ideal theme is not a typal conception or an archetype that establishes a pattern of behavior. A vision of an ideal theme focuses upon the total character of a way of life. It does not function as a sketch governing the making of programs or blueprints for moral behavior. As a telos of a style of life, an ideal theme functions as a standard of inspiration, not by providing an articulate norm to be complied with, but by providing a *point of orientation.* A moral agent regards his ideal theme more like an apex, so to speak, of a divergent series of values without a subsumptive scheme. The ideal theme is like a fixed star in which the agent directs his attention and his actions revolve. An ideal norm typically functions as a standard of aspiration which issues in a sense of moral progress in one's efforts toward ideal achievement (Section 7B). With an ideal theme, on the other hand, moral progress is measured not in terms of compliance with a norm but rather in terms of the degree of *comportment* with the ideal focus.

The basic difficulty in making clear the notion of ideal themes lies perhaps in the indeterminacy of meaning in our ideal vocabulary. Terms such as love, justice, benevolence, and compassion appear to admit of both a normative and thematic interpretation, depending on the attitude of the reflective moral agent. For some agents they may be understood as ideal themes that form the points of focal reference and orientation for conduct without issuing normative directives. We have occasionally taken note of Christian *agape* and Confucian *jên* as ideal themes. Perhaps we can also construe the Good of Plato and the State of Beatitude and Blessedness of Aquinas as ideal themes rather than norms. We think also of Zen's *Satori* and the *Tao* of Lao-tzu and Chuang-tzu as visions of ideal themes. We have no special vocabulary for ideal themes. The main point lies in stressing a different way of interpreting moral ideals as having an important consequence in understanding a dimension of moral creativity.

In our attempted explication, we may take the Good of Plato, Christian *agape,* Confucian *jên* as paradigms for understanding ideal themes as quasi-aesthetic visions. All these ideal notions are infected with vagueness. Adopting a term from Wheelwright, we may regard ideal themes in general as *plurisignations*—a term used earlier in connection with our discussion on Confucian ethics. According to Wheelwright, "Apart from any question of whether or not its meanings are altered by shifting context, an expressive symbol tends on any occasion of its realization, to carry more than one legitimate reference—or if not something definite enough to be called a reference, then at least more than one legitimate group of connotations and suggestions—in such a way that its full meaning involves a tension between two or more directions of semantic stress."[9] For our purpose a plurisignative notion may be regarded as a notion that possesses as it were a power to suggest and stimulate different thoughts and interpretations. So construed as plurisignations, ideal themes such as Platonic Good and *agape* do not admit of a unitary interpretation and description apart from the conception and conduct of reflective agents. An ideal theme is a quasi-aesthetic vision, a telos of a style of life to be developed with no a priori directive guidance. Plato, for instance, did not offer us a definition of the Good, nor Jesus "Love thy Neighbor," nor Confucius *jên.* Plato, in the *Republic,* drew an analogy between the Good and the Sun. Just as the Sun is responsible for the existence and growth of things, the Good is responsible for the existence and illumination of the Forms. The Good is a sort of focal point or reference in which moral activities converge. The achievement of the Good thus gives an illuminating and pervasive quality to one's moral life. The Good, taken as an ideal theme, has a focal unity, but it does not provide directives to conduct. If the analogy between the Good and the Sun is to be taken seriously, one can have the Good as an ideal theme without the necessity of having an epistemology of moral ideals. (This discussion, inspired by Plato's analogy in Book VI of the *Republic,* is not intended as an adequate account of the doctrine of forms.)

A quasi-aesthetic vision remains an intellectual conception. Its unity is a unity of focus. And for a commitive agent, it is a point of orientation to which his conduct *comports* rather than a sketch with determinable blueprints. So construed, an ideal theme, when assented to, is a theme to be developed. Actions that comport with an ideal theme may have enormous diversity. An achieved theme is an achieved quality of moral excellence, giving a significance to the life of the moral agent who lives it. Prospectively, a theme to be developed admits of a diversity of idiosyncratic achievements. Being plurisignative, an ideal theme does not prejudge the nature of the corresponding developed state.

This is its essential indeterminacy in meaning, which yields a polymorphous achievement of moral creativity.

As a telos of a style of life, an ideal theme may be the target of ritual or ceremonial acts. This is the peculiar stress of Confucian *li*. How a theme is developed does not depend on the descriptive content of performance, but rather on the spirit and style in which actions are performed. In Confucian ethics, it is the active commitment to *jên* as an ideal theme that prevents *li* and styles of performance from degenerating into mere habitual routines (Section 4B). The *point* of performing rituals can easily be forgotten, thus divesting actions of their ideal focus and their moral vitality. The morality of the styles of performance lies in the ideal theme that illuminates them. Without the *jên* spirit, styles of performance would be mere manners of behavior devoid of moral significance.

B. Ideal Norms and Ideal Themes: Some Dimensions of Contrast

In this section we briefly discuss some possible dimensions of contrast between ideal norms and ideal themes.

Attitude toward the question of being.   In Section 6G we noted that the question "What shall I be?" depending on the agent's attitude, could be interpreted as a problem indicator or as a perplexity indicator calling for an ideal answer. An ideal norm may be regarded as an answer to a problem indicator. Thus the question of being or of what sort of a moral person one wants to be may be interpreted as a problem of seeking an answer in terms of an ideal norm that will guide prospectively in one's chosen way of life. Ideal norms as answers to problem indicators provide standards of moral excellence for solutions to the agent's predicament. In this way, an agent's moral predicament is viewed as a setting for a normative problem that admits of conceptual formulation. So construed, the question of being admits of rational and objective consideration. Normative ethical theories may be profitably construed as attempts to furnish rational solutions to the question of being as a problem indicator. What is of interest from the theoretical point of view is the manner in which a question can be dealt with as a problem apart from the peculiar setting of individual agents' intentions and purposes. As a problem, it is treated as pervasive of a common predicament of moral agents. From this point of view, the orbit of personal intentions drops out of consideration, for the canons of objectivity and rationality that guide our theoretic inquiry have no reference to personal intentions. Of course, a personal question can occur merely as a personal problem to which ideal norms may be offered as possible solutions. In this individual setting, the question of being may be regarded by the agent as a personal problem indicator that calls for an ideal answer without claim to universality and prescriptivity to all moral agents. It cannot be denied, moreover, that a personal problem can have a public significance in the sense that it may depict a common predicament of problematic situations to which ideal norms offer a directive guidance.

An agent, being in a state of perplexity, may try to see clearly the sort of issue or problem that confronts him. Assuming that he fails to locate and formulate a problem that can be handled in some objective fashion, but he is convinced that his perplexity is a meaningful one and admits of some sort of an answer (though not the sort of answer that would solve an articulated problem), his question may then be regarded as a perplexity indicator—a perplexity that does not admit of a problematic formulation and solution. The question of being may thus be regarded as a perplexity indicator that calls for an answer in terms of an ideal theme rather than an ideal norm. The question is, as I have suggested, a search for an ideal quality of life that will endow one's life with a meaning or significance. It must be observed that the experience of a perplexity indicator that resists problematical formulation is certainly not an ordinary occurrence. It does not depict a normal situation of human life as we know it. However, it may occur in some moral agent's life in the experience of "crisis of values" as a crisis that is not directed to the solution of particular problems. Jung stresses this sort of crisis that often occurs in a man's middle life. "The nearer we approach to the middle of life [between thirty-five and forty years of age], and the better we have succeeded in entrenching ourselves in our personal attitudes and social positions, the more it appears as if we had discovered the right course and the right ideals and principles of behavior. For this reason we suppose them to be eternally valid, and make a virtue of unchangeably clinging to them. We overlook the essential fact that the social goal is attained only at the cost of a diminution of personality."[10] If this sort of crisis is viewed as a moral crisis that addresses the need of an ideal answer, the moral agent's quest, if successful, may be an answer in terms of an ideal theme rather than an ideal norm. The quest is a quest for a quality of life rather than an ideal norm that measures one's moral achievement. The quest of being, even if it fails or provides no satisfactory answer to the agent concerned, may still be a meaningful question that opens up a wider and deeper dimension of moral consciousness in the very process of struggle with the perplexity indicator. Here we learn from creative writers and artists. "The writer and the artist are not presenting answers but creating as an experience of something in themselves trying to work—to seek, to find and not to yield. The contribution which is given to the world by the painting or the book is the process of the search."[11]

Knowledge. We may also contrast ideal norms with ideal themes in terms of two different sorts of moral knowledge that an agent may be said to possess. Adopting a distinction of Russell's, we may say that an ideal norm is an object of descriptive knowledge rather than of acquaintance.[12] An agent having an ideal norm must know how to articulate its nature in terms of a set of propositions forming, as it were, the blueprints for actions. This sort of knowledge is something that an agent can have prior to any actual performance. Compliance with an ideal norm presupposes the norm as an epistemic object *anterior* to performance. As suggested toward the end of Section 2C, this sort of knowledge is not affected or altered by actions. An ideal theme, on the other hand, is more of an object of acquaintance. We may compare an ideal theme to the archer's target. An archer may know his target without being able to articulate the descriptive content of the target. An ideal theme, as a focal point of orientation, is a telos or target of moral achievement. The descriptive nature of the target cannot be spelled out in advance of the actions and efforts of the agent in the process of realizing his ideal theme. The descriptive knowledge is, so to speak, *posterior* rather than anterior to performance. Nevertheless, an ideal theme is an object of knowledge by *acquaintance.* One may know by acquaintance the nature of an ideal theme prior to performance, just as one person may know or recognize another person without knowing that certain descriptions apply to him. In like manner, a painter may know what it is he wants to paint without knowing descriptively what the finished product will look like. The process of painting is in this manner a process of creative discovery of the descriptive constituents of the artist's conception. With ideal theme, the process of realization may also be regarded as a process of creative discovery.[13] A developed ideal theme is a species of moral achievement.

Strategy.   We may also contrast ideal norms with ideal themes in terms of the nature of the means employed. When an agent knows descriptively the nature of his ideal norm, his strategic problem is to find the means that will be the effective instruments in achieving his end. Instrumental means in this way are extrinsic to the nature of ideal norms. This is not to deny that some instrumental means may become parts of an achieved moral state. If an agent, for instance, while employing a means in his ideal pursuit, experiences consummatory satisfaction in some of his actions, his means may become a constitutive feature of his moral achievement through the process of habituation.[14] Something that is first desired as an instrumental means can thus become an ingredient in moral achievement. However, when an agent commits himself to an ideal norm, his problem of execution is primarily a problem of moral engineering, i.e., a technical problem of finding effective means for applying the norm to practice. In the case of an ideal theme, the strategic problem for a commitive agent is to find the kind of means that are pervaded by the quality of his vision. We may call these "qualitative means." The problem is not a technical one of finding appropriate techniques for realization of an ideal, but more like the problem of an artist seeking the appropriate medium and materials for the execution of his plan. And when an artist succeeds in his search, both the medium and materials are pervaded with the quality which he originally conceives. In like manner, the qualitative means are uniquely constitutive of an agent's ideal achievement. An agent's life, for example, pervaded with a *jên* quality or an *agape* quality, can be seen to be one in which the ideal theme *diffuses* through the various activities of life. The search for qualitative means is a search for means that will form an intrinsic part of one's moral life. The qualitative means belong in the domain of polymorphous moral creativity.

The role of paradigmatic individuals.   The question of intrinsic actuation of moral knowledge and practice, which occasioned this inquiry, is a question that concerns the transforming significance of morality (Chapter 2). This question, in the context of a reflective agent's quest for being, can be seen as an ideal question that addresses itself to a moral practice. Insofar as an agent sees his moral practice as embedded with an ideal which he regards as a satisfactory answer to his quest, his acceptance of the moral practice would be an ideal acceptance. If the ideal be an ideal norm, the norm would function as a standard for measuring his conduct and so acquire a justificatory import in his life.

However, a moral agent can look to other agents for guidance insofar as these agents share the same ideal norm and appear to have embodied it in some exemplary fashion in their lives and conduct. These exemplary agents may thus acquire a standard-guiding function *derivative* from the ideal norm. They may become objects of emulation or personal models for imitation. But for these exemplary agents not to remain as mere extrinsic actuations of an ideal norm, they must appear to the commitive agent as standards of inspiration, as possessing an active and dynamic force—an intrinsically actuating force of a moral ideal. An exemplary agent in this sense is a paradigmatic individual who serves as an example of an intrinsic actuation of a moral ideal. It is not denied here that for pedagogical purposes, moral teachers often regard paradigmatic individuals as illustrations of how moral ideals can be achieved. But as mere illustrations, citation of paradigmatic individuals remains an extrinsic feature of a moral ideal. They cannot provide standards of inspiration for the lives of the moral learners. A model for imitation remains a static rather than an inspiring example of a moral ideal. It is the model that, so to speak, infuses an ideal norm with an active force that can serve a paradigmatic function for other commitive agents.

One moral agent often regards another as an exemplar of an ideal norm by projecting certain qualities onto that person without that person actually possessing them. Hartmann reminds us that "a positive example is not something taken wholly from actual experience. We project the pattern upon a real person, or we idealize the person, and thus he becomes an exemplar."[15] However, an exemplary agent taken in this way must be regarded as a *live* person rather than a mere archetypical conception. We idealize other living persons and regard them as exemplars only insofar as we encounter them as persons with the same ideal concern who, in our view, however partial and inadequate, to some extent embody the ideal norm. We may, owing to our ignorance, project ideal features onto such a person's life without his actually possessing them. This ideal projection is perhaps inevitable with historical paradigms who lived in a different age and cultural epoch since we do not now possess what can be regarded as uncontrovertible pieces of authentic biographical evidence. What needs to be recognized for our purpose is the way in which these paradigmatic persons function as guides to conduct in different moral practices. Admittedly, their standard-guiding role derives from commitment to an ideal norm. Noting this derivative status, however, does not deprive them from being examples of intrinsic actuation of moral ideals, and of being in themselves standards of inspiration.

A moral agent, of course, need not take other agents as exemplars of his ideal achievement. He may merely conceive of an ideal type of man that satisfies the requirements of his ideal norm. As a mere conception, this ideal man can still function as a guiding archetype and as a standard for measuring achievement. Kant construes the Stoic ideal of a wise man in this way: "The wise man [of the Stoics] is . . . an ideal, that is, a man existing in thought only, but in complete conformity with the idea of wisdom. As the idea gives the *rule,* so the ideal in such a case serves as the *archetype* for the complete determination of the copy; and we have no other standard for our actions than the conduct of this divine man within us, with which we compare and judge ourselves, and so reform ourselves, although we can never attain to the perfection thereby prescribed."[16] As a conceptual archetype, moreover, it can provide no dynamics of its own apart from an agent's active commitment to its realization in practice. It is more of an object of wish rather than an object of inspiration unless one can appeal to some living exemplars who endow the archetype with an intrinsically active force. But if there are such exemplars, the conceived archetype has no dynamic role to play since it is the ideal norm that seeks an expression in life. What can furnish a *home* for this ideal is the living agents who embody it rather than a mere theoretic embodiment in reason.

We have observed that paradigmatic individuals are standards of inspiration in various moral practices. Their exemplary moral achievement is inspiring in the style in which they orient themselves toward their moral practices and ideals (Section 3C). The focal point of their standard-guiding function thus lies in their styles of life rather than in their embodiment of ideals abstractly conceived. This is particularly the case with ideal themes. When an individual embodies an ideal theme his style of life must display a quality that diffuses throughout his conduct. It is this diffused and pervasive quality that perhaps inspires other agents in their striving for ideal achievement. A paradigmatic individual can in this way be a standard of inspiration—a focal point of orientation for other agents. In the case of ideal norms, we should note that certain agents, though not regarded by others as a total embodiment of an ideal, can also serve as exemplary guides to others by embodying particular excellences in their various pieces of conduct. If we regard virtues in general as commendatory styles of performance, these virtues may be viewed as embodiments of instrumental means for ideal achievement. Moral heroes, saints, and obscure exemplary agents in any moral practice may serve to guide others in a partial sense of having fulfilled some parts of the requirement of the ideal norm. With an ideal theme, the embodiment of qualitative means in persons can also be regarded as a partial embodiment detached from the focal point of reference. Virtues can be admired and can also inspire ideal achievement when they are viewed as constitutive features of an achieved state of a person. However, detached from the governing guide of moral ideals, virtues are more objects of praise that may not possess a transforming significance for moral agents.

Since an ideal norm is a standard of measure, it has a justificatory import for a commitive agent. An agent may appeal to his ideal norm in justifying particular pieces of conduct. A paradigmatic individual can in this sense function as a derivative justificatory standard. With an ideal theme, on the other hand, a paradigmatic individual functions more as a standard of intrinsic actuation than as a standard for justification. The paradigmatic individual inspires an ideal task without being an object of aspiration. An ideal theme has concrete significance only when it is developed by a moral agent. There can be no substitute for autonomous self-development. Paradigmatic individuals provide exemplars, but no recipes for moral creativity.

Answers to the question of being. Two observations must be made concerning the distinction between ideal norms and ideal themes as answers to the question of being. First, resolving a perplexity indicator does not entail a resolution of all moral problems, nor does finding an ideal norm as an answer to a problem indicator entail the extinction or resolution of all moral dilemmas. And, second, given ideal norm—which all moral agents agree is embedding a moral practice—may be viewed by a particular agent as having an import only as an ideal theme. The first observation is an important qualification. A satisfactory answer to a perplexity indicator does not solve all moral problems. An ideal theme, as I have frequently stressed, is a point of orientation, not a method for resolving problems. It is a moral perspective in light of which problems are to be resolved, but not a perspective one can look to for preceptorial guidance. A preoccupation with moral problems is a continuing concern regardless of one's ideal theme. The problems of acting are a fact of moral life. No ideal theme can transform this fact into an illusion. Likewise, having an ideal norm as an answer to a problem indicator does not entail the resolution of all moral perplexities. As a telos of a way of life, an ideal norm is not free from perplexing questioning about its quality and import. A man who succeeds in fulfilling his ideal norm may come to question its transforming significance for his future life. He may come to regard his way of life as devoid of qualitative significance, thus subjecting his life to a searching scrutiny. He may be in search of a style of life dominated by an ideal theme.

Both ideal themes and ideal norms are moral perspectives that may conflict in actual cases. The possibility of their conflict is a warning of the inadequacy of any a priori assimilation of one to the other. Our second observation relates to the first. Since both ideal norms and ideal themes share a common vocabulary, there is no a priori way of determining the import of moral ideals. We can suggest a practical test: Is an ideal, e.g., love or justice, viewed by the moral agent as a telos of his way of life or as a telos of his style of life? The former would be an ideal norm, and the latter an ideal theme. But it remains the case that what is an ideal norm for one person may be an ideal theme to another. There is no meaningful a priori determination of the nature of an agent's commitment. Only the agent can provide an adequate answer to our question.

C. Philosophic Import of the Distinction

If the distinction between ideal norm and ideal theme as set forth in the preceding sections is adjudged to be tolerably clear, an important question arises concerning the philosophical significance of this distinction. Before we tackle this difficult question, a few remarks should be made on how the distinction is to be evaluated. For one thing, the distinction proposed is a distinction between two interpretations of moral ideals from the point of view of a reflective moral agent. It is not intended as a categorial distinction that enables one to classify moral ideals. It is intended as a distinction that in some ways helps us in our attempt to understand the ideal dimension of creative agency. Its only claim to importance thus lies in its capacity to discern the nature of moral ideals in terms of their import for moral agents in general and, ultimately, to that difficult question on the meaning of one's life. With regard to the latter question, the relevance of our distinction of moral ideals implies no claim to providing an answer, for in the final analysis, that question calls for an individual decision.

Recent moral philosophy is not much concerned with moral ideals.

In a sense, this is intelligible, for, unlike moral rules, moral ideals do not seem to admit of conceptual analysis. Their essential vagueness and seeming arbitrary subjectivity do not encourage conceptual interest. Hare and Strawson did pay some attention to moral ideals; however, they tend toward the notion of ideal norms rather than ideal themes. Consequently an important aspect of the function of moral ideals is neglected. In this way, our proposed distinction may be regarded as an attempt to fill an important gap in understanding moral ideals. The question properly arises: How does this distinction between ideal norms and ideal themes help one to understand a dimension of creative agency? One answer lies in appreciating the role of paradigmatic individuals who actuate the ideals, thus enlivening the ideals with a vitality all their own. They furnish the concrete locus in which mere ideals become real possibilities of achievement. And this role can be viewed in terms of embodiment either of an ideal norm or of an ideal theme. Of course, the inspiring role of paradigmatic individuals does not guarantee actual realization of ideals, for any concrete piece of realization depends on the character, ability, opportunity, and depth of commitment to these ideals. Ordinary moral agents, though inspired by the paradigmatic individuals, can have a creative role to play in their ideal-governed and ideal-styled conduct. Through their ideal rulings, moral agents also may acquire paradigmatic status for the lives and conduct of other agents. Their concern and active willing of ideal conduct are a dimension for *appreciating* their idiosyncratic contributions, particularly in the realm of ideal themes. Of course, these contributions are subject to public assessment insofar as their descriptive content is concerned. Being problem-oriented persons, we tend to stress the conflict between ideal norms, rather than the harmony of moral ideal and rules in individual pieces of conduct. As previously observed (Section 7B), commitment to a moral practice may be carried out in light of this ideal. This is particularly noteworthy in the case of an ideal theme. Our distinction between ideal norms and ideal themes enables us to focus on the intimate link between ideals and rules within the life of some moral agents. The recognition of this possibility, particularly in the case of ideal themes, offers us a wider dimension for understanding moral creativity.

A focus on paradigmatic individuals as embodiments of ideal norms and themes also reminds us of the possibility of shared visions and ways of life, enabling us to understand moral creativity in the manner in which a personal vision can acquire interpersonal significance. This observation, of course, does not foreclose the need for an independent examination of their justificatory status. In themselves ideal norms are subject to rational and reasonable assessment. We can assess them in terms of consistency and coherence of articulation and this can further be assessed in terms of the agent's conception of their reflective desirability. When an ideal norm is advocated and accepted, it has a sort of universality antecedent to performance. In the case of an ideal theme, when it is shared and accepted by moral agents it is again subject to an assessment in terms of reflective desirability. When such an assessment is accepted, it has a sort of universality too, a universality consequent upon their accepted paradigmatic status. This issue in the epistemology of morals goes beyond our present scope. We merely are content to focus on the issue as it bears on our concern with moral creativity.

For the most part we have focused upon the subjective nature of ideal themes. It may be objected that if ideal themes are thus "subjectively" located, why emphasize them? Why should other agents bother with one's thematic concern? Is the appreciation of another person's ideal theme a legitimate interest of moral agents in general? I think it is an important interest, since an ideal theme if developed can acquire a power of contagion. Subjectivity neither divests it of possible charm and attraction nor prevents it from being an object of admiration if not inspiration. To use Hutcheson's term, individual moral sentiment is here an "approving faculty." And when an ideal theme is approved of, it can be a basis for "election"; and when a person is deeply committed to it, it can bring a qualitative dimension to his moral life. And when that person becomes paradigmatic, his life of diffusive quality may inspire others and may even invest a moral practice with a new character and function. The moral life would be the poorer without ideal themes, just as our social life would be the poorer without ideal norms. Here we merely enter a conviction. There is always an option open to a moral agent to reject its importance. But who but a reflective moral agent can decide this question of importance?

The preceding remarks I hope offer some reasonable considerations for the acceptance of the distinction made in this book. My aim has been to focus on the ideal dimension of moral creativity without pretending to offer a philosophical account of the nature of moral ideals. I offer no value scheme for moral agents, but merely point out the possible forms and consequences of our focus in an attempt to understand the moral life. I have not attempted to reduce the dynamic complexity of moral creativity to some methodically manageable outline.

The distinction between ideal norm and ideal theme represents another experiment in understanding moral creativity. In spite of this distinction, the two are not precluded from having an intimate connection within the life of a moral agent. As a consequence of experience and reflection an ideal norm may be transformed into a theme without a corresponding change in linguistic expression. Suppose we assume that an agent commits himself to *agape* initially as a normative principle of benevolence; he may on reflection regard this principle as simply one of the alternative interpretations of *agape*, thus imbuing his original understanding of *agape* with a thematic concern. *Agape* now has become a theme, with the principle of benevolence regarded as one among diverse possible developments of a moral ideal. In this way, a moral agent may be concerned not merely with the active promotion of the welfare of others but also with the quality of welfare-inducing performance. Similarly, a Confucian agent who takes *jên* as a supreme norm of conduct within a ritual system (*li*) may on reflection transform *jên* into an ideal theme, with the system of *li* as one possible expression, thus allowing *jên* to have an import quite independent of its tie with *li*. In this way an ideal norm can serve as a ground, admittedly contingent, for the conception of an ideal theme. Moreover, an ideal theme can also serve as a ground for the inception of an ideal norm. A Confucian who initially commits himself to *jên* as an ideal theme may on reflection realize that such a theme cannot be concretely developed apart from having a tie to a moral practice pervaded by *li*. Thus *jên* as an ideal theme becomes in this way dependent for its actualization upon compliance with an existing normative system. Further, he may come to conceive this normative system as being capable of a thematic infusion, thus achieving a sort of fusion of ideal theme and norm. The question of priority of ground and consequence is thus contingent upon the agent's conception of the import of moral ideals to the question of meaning in *his* life. When this question is a problem indicator, ideal norms are more likely to win his allegiance and serve as a possible ground for an ideal theme. When the question is a perplexity indicator, ideal themes are bound to be more appropriate and persuasive answers and can serve as a possible ground for an ideal norm. And when both ideal norms and themes appear to join in a friendly relationship, the agent can experience their affinity and harmony. The distinction between ideal norm and theme is then understood in light of their connection. Reflection on the nature of one's ideal commitments is therefore a continuing task of moral agency.

D. Recapitulation and Further Task

We began our exploration from the *position* of a reflective agent concerned with understanding moral creativity. This concern we conceived to be an expression of an interest in the problem of creative agency within a moral practice. The problem is the *possibility* of creative individual contributions to a moral practice viewed in light of a commitive moral agent. After a preliminary discussion of the nature of our approach in Chapter 1, we discussed a question on actuation of moral theory and practice. This question, I believe, cannot be theoretically answered, for it does not appear to be the sort of question that has a clear sense amenable to a theoretical treatment. However, we assumed that the question is intelligible and attempted to formulate it as a question of intrinsic rather than extrinsic actuation of moral theory and practice. The question of intrinsic actuation, in the final analysis, turns out to be a question on the transforming significance of morality.

In considering the question of intrinsic actuation a philosopher can point to paradigmatic individuals who exemplify the intrinsic actuations of moral practices. Chapter 3 explored the significance of the notion of paradigmatic individuals. An extensive excursion into Confucian ethics, stressing the centrality of the notion of paradigmatic individuals in both Confucian teaching and practice, followed. The two chapters on Confucian ethics thus furnish a concrete habitat for the notion of paradigmatic individuals. We also noted the distinctive feature of Confucian ethics as an ethics of flexibility with a stress on reasonable moral agents within the Confucian moral tradition.

In a way, we may now view the three chapters on the notion of paradigmatic individuals as an attempt to set forth a prototype for understanding creative moral agency. The usefulness of this notion in part lies in the provision of an answer to our original question on the *possibility* of moral creativity within a moral practice. Greater and lesser paradigmatic individuals in different moral practices do exemplify the *manners* in which individual moral agents invest existing moral practices with a new character and function. If the paradigmatic individuals are exemplars of intrinsic actuation, their manner of orientation to their moral practices also has a transforming effect on preestablished moralities. We believe that a further study of the paradigmatic individuals will furnish an illuminating view of the dynamics of existing moralities. Thus our chapters on paradigmatic individuals may be regarded as a discussion on a dimension of moral creativity that focuses upon the root possibility of moral creativity itself. We may now call this the *exemplary* dimension of moral creativity.

In Chapter 6 we turned to the discussion of moral rules and rulings and attempted to expound features of moral creativity within a moral practice. The problem of moral creativity was discussed in terms of the relevance of moral rules to particular circumstances that beset individual agents. We focused on the reconstitutive character of a moral practice in relation to an individual agent's conception of his problematic predicament. Our discussion here may be summed up in terms of a focus on the *reconstitutive* dimension of moral creativity.

Our journey into moral rules and rulings culminated in a stress on a different dimension of ruling that is not necessarily tied to a moral practice. We distinguished between problem indicators and perplexity indicators and their possible answers in terms of ideal norms and ideal themes which respectively constitute the targets of achievement of ways and styles of life. In this way we focused on the *ideal* dimension to which we devoted the last two chapters.

Throughout our journey, we employed a variety of focal notions in order to lay stress on the exemplary, reconstitutive, and ideal dimensions of moral creativity. By way of conclusion, let us reiterate a basic point in our inquiry. I have not attempted to furnish an account or a theory of moral creativity. Rather, this book is an attempt to understand, not by way of a theory, but by way of suggestive models that offer an insight into the dynamics of the valuative life of moral agents. The focal notions of form of life, way of life, and style of life are emphasized and arguments for their significance in understanding moral creativity are presented. I have, in effect, attempted to exhibit these focal notions, though not in systematic form, and to propose plausible suggestions and arguments for their significance for both moral theory and practice. The problem of moral creativity, like artistic creativity, is, of course, not amenable to philosophical theoretical construction. My aim has been, to adopt a phrase of Wittgenstein's, to assemble reminders for the purpose of understanding moral creativity. This enterprise is basically an enterprise in self-understanding that can only suggest that other agents agree *reflectively* that the features we focused on are of central importance to their own attempts at self-understanding. For moral philosophy, our focal notions perhaps offer grounds for the possibility of their use in intimating, suggesting, or adumbrating models for an adequate understanding of moral life as a whole. The notion of a way of life does suggest a model for understanding the sense or cognitive aspect of moral experience in terms of rationality and *reasonability*. The notion of a style of life suggests a model for understanding the aspect of *responsive sensibility* of moral agency. However, the notion of a form of life does not suggest any model, but rather is a mere focal lens to draw attention to the presupposition in understanding the moral life. I hope our inquiry has a bearing on the philosopher's central concern with the epistemology of morals by suggesting that our notions of a way or style of life offer a base for understanding moral justification. We may say here that any attempt to understand the moral life as a whole, inclusive of claims to justification, requires a *cooperation* between rather than a division of *reason* and *sentiment*. This is a tribute we pay to the contributions of eighteenth-century British Moralists without joining in the issue that separates them, for the two models we offer for understanding morality are complementary rather than exclusive models. They assemble complementary reminders for a cognitive sympathetic understanding of the moral life. This naturally leaves the question of assessment of moral commitments as a separate inquiry. I hope this book will serve as a groundwork for the construction of a theory of moral justifications.

Notes

Complete references can be found in the Bibliography following these Notes.

Introduction

1. Hare, *Language of Morals,* ch. IV.
2. Ibid., 65.
3. Mayo, *Ethics and the Moral Life,* 193.
4. J.O. Urmson, "Saints and Heroes," in Melden, *Essays in Moral Philosophy,* 198–216; Horsburgh, "The Plurality of Moral Standards," 332–46.
5. Strawson, "Social Morality and Individual Ideal," in Ramsey, *Christian Ethics,* 280–98. See also Hare, *Freedom and Reason,* for a later recognition of the role of ideals in understanding morality.
6. Iris Murdoch, "Vision and Choice in Morality," in Ramsey, *Christian Ethics,* 202.
7. Helen Oppenheimer, "Moral Choice and Divine Authority," in Ramsey, *Christian Ethics,* 221.
8. Ibid., 223.
9. See Hart, *The Concept of Law,* 86 and 244. In Sections 6A and 6B we explore the nature of a moral practice and the relation between the internal and external points of view of a moral practice within the context of agency.

Chapter 1

1. I do not intend this distinction between cartography and epistemology of morals to be a categorial distinction that precludes any possible sort of relations. The distinction is offered to mark a difference in pragmatic aims and directions of inquiry, and not as a distinction that can serve as a basis for classifying ethical theories. A comprehensive cartography of morals is likely to involve difficult epistemological issues, particularly in terms of assessment of its claim to provide an adequate structure of moral experiences in general. A selective cartography of morals, however, is more modest in its epistemological pretensions, since it does not claim to have discovered universal truths. In this sense, it has no epistemological thesis to offer, though its results, if accepted, can provide a basis for constructing an epistemological theory of morals. In any case, the two enterprises are related; however, their difference is a central concern. I hope to explore this problem in a future work on moral justification.
2. In addition to the three terms to be discussed I employ a family of focal notions, e.g., actuation, paradigmatic individual, problem indicator and perplexity indicator, ideal norms and ideal themes. All these notions will receive greater elaboration as we progress toward the end of the exploration. What Ruth Saw regards as aesthetic concepts applies to our focal notions: "The point of concepts used in aesthetic discourse is to direct our attention to the important features of the work. These features are important in the sense that if they were not noticed, the work would not be appreciated." *Aesthetics,* 197.

3. Wittgenstein, *Philosophical Investigations,* 226. There is a variety of interpretations of Wittgenstein's notion of forms of life. For some recent accounts, see the essays by J.F.M. Hunter and F. Zabeeh in E.D. Klemke, ed., *Essays on Wittgenstein.* The use here is not intended as another interpretation of Wittgenstein but is, I hope, sufficiently clear without ascribing the use to Wittgenstein. Part of Chapter 6 is devoted to a more elaborate discussion of this notion.

4. Kovesi, *Moral Notions,* 51, 109, 121, 142.

5. Austin, "How to Talk," in *Philosophical Papers,* 189.

6. Hampshire, *Freedom of Mind,* 55–56. This incidentally is the import of the Confucian doctrine of "rectifying names" discussed in Section 5B.

7. I am familiar with this experience of culture shock which is pervasive among well-educated Chinese in the Philippines. While these Chinese live within the Confucian atmosphere at home, when they go to Western schools and engage in various occupations they confront an entirely alien form of life. Their existence is as it were transformed onto a different plane. They experience culture shock. Many overseas Chinese live a sort of schizophrenic existence. Each of them does not live two entirely different ways of life, but each lives a way of life that ambiguously anchors upon two different forms of life.

8. Russell, *Problems of Philosophy,* ch. 5.

9. These remarks on the form of life as the lived background of a moral practice may bring more obscurity than clarity to the use of this notion. It seems that what requires emphasis in understanding moral creativity is the existential background that renders such creativity possible and meaningful. The background is the presupposition of both moral discourse and performance. A reflective agent may try to articulate this background in some conceptual form, but this would introduce a definite view on the nature of the background which may be incompatible with the views of other agents. I leave the philosophic and moral import of this possibility open. Some of my colleagues would insist on the necessity of some sort of metaphysical account, but I merely focus on the necessity of recognizing this lived background without prejudging its ontological significance. Perhaps our discussion of the notion of a way of life will provide a clearer contrast to the notion of the form of life. It is quite common in recent literature to use the two notions interchangeably. But it seems important to distinguish them: whereas a form of life cannot conceptually be formulated, ways of life can be explicated in conceptual terms.

10. For the most part I use the term "moral practice" rather than "communal or cultural way of life." I sometimes use the term "moral community" with the same purport. Where I use the term "ways of life," the focus is on individual rather than communal mode of existence. Further elaborations are found in Sections 6A and 7D.

11. Whiteley, "On Defining 'moral,' " in Wallace and Walker, *The Definition of Morality,* 22.

12. Taylor, *Normative Discourse,* 135.

13. Watson, *Hsün Tzu,* 88–111.

14. Kroeber, *Style of Civilizations,* 70–71.

15. See von Wright, *Explanation and Understanding,* 134. Cf. Rescher, *Conceptual Idealism,* 189–94.

16. Kierkegaard, *The Concept of Dread,* 127.

Chapter 2

1. Hume, *Principles of Morals,* 5.

2. Kant, *Lectures on Ethics,* 36. It should be noted that Kant did not use this terminology in his critical ethical writings.

3. Gilbert Ryle, "Conscience and Moral Conviction," in MacDonald, *Philosophy and Analysis,* 159.

4. Moore, *Principia Ethica,* ch. 1, sec. 4. For a recent discussion of the importance of casuistry, see Henry Margenau, *Ethics and Science,* 158ff.

5. Bentham, *Morals and Legislation,* 24, 25.

6. Mill, *Utilitarianism,* 35–36.

7. Ibid., 34.

8. Shaftesbury, *Virtue or Merit,* 1:292.

9. Hume, *Principles of Morals,* 45.

10. Mill, *Utilitarianism,* 40, 37.

11. Hume, *Principles of Morals,* 45, 49, 59, 120.

12. For the distinction between logical and real or ingredient possibility, see Weiss, *Modes of Being,* sec. 2.13.

13. Beck, *Commentary,* 212.

14. Kant, *Critique of Practical Reason,* 75.

15. Kant, *Foundations of the Metaphysics of Morals,* 17.

16. Pepper, *World Hypotheses,* ch. 5.

17. "Meaning is a physiognomy." Wittgenstein, *Philosophical Investigations,* 1:568.

18. See Downie, "Roles and Moral Agency."

19. Hume, *Principles of Morals,* 88–89.

20. Hampshire, "J.L. Austin," ii.

21. Schopenhauer, "Studies in Pessimism," in *Essays,* 138. Italics mine.

22. Kierkegaard, *Concluding Unscientific Postscript,* 150–51. Italics mine.

Chapter 3

1. Hare, *The Language of Morals,* 69.

2. Kai Nielsen, "Why Should I Be Moral?," in Taylor, *Problems of Moral Philosophy,* 516.

3. All quotations from Jaspers cited in the text are from *Socrates, Buddha, Confucius, and Jesus.*

4. Wheelwright, *Heraclitus,* 14.

5. Wittgenstein, *Philosophical Investigations,* pt. I, 19, 23.

6. *Symposium,* 216e–217a. Translated by Michael Joyce in Hamilton and Cairn, *Collected Dialogues of Plato.* Cf. Lao Tzu, ch. 70: "The Sage wears coarse clothes while keeping the jade in his bosom." *Lao Tzu: Tao Teh Ching,* trans. J.C.H. Wu.

7. Tucker, "Theory of Charismatic Leadership," 737.

8. Aristotle, *Nicomachean Ethics,* bk. X, 1179a, 15–20.

9. Warnock, *Contemporary Moral Philosophy,* 64.

10. Chan, *Reflections on Things at Hand,* 76.

11. Berkeley, *A Treatise Concerning the Principles of Human Knowledge,* in Luce and Jessop, ed., *The Works of George Berkeley,* Vol. II. Introduction, para. 12, para. 15.

12. Ibid., 128.

13. Bergson, *Two Sources of Morality and Religion,* 43. For a recent discussion of this distinction independent of Bergson, see Fuller, *The Morality of Law,* ch. 1.

14. Bergson, *Two Sources of Morality and Religion,* 42.

15. Hartmann, *Ethics,* 1:195.
16. Horsburgh, "The Plurality of Moral Standards," 336.

Chapter 4

1. In Cua, "The Logic of Confucian Dialogues" I attempted to set forth a conceptual map for the *Analects* based on a discussion of certain characteristic uses of general remarks. See also Holzman, "The Conversational Tradition in Chinese Philosophy."
2. Creel, *Confucius and the Chinese Way,* 137.
3. Hummel, "Some Basic Moral Principles in Chinese Culture," 601. This remark does not of course apply to the People's Republic of China. However, Confucian ethics continues to exert influence among non-Communist Chinese around the world.
4. Some recent scholars' claim that Confucian ethics is relevant to present-day problems may be found in James R. Ware's introduction to his translation of the *Analects,* 7, and Wu-chi Liu's *A Short History of Confucian Philosophy,* 11.
5. Because of the lack of equivalent appraisive concepts in English I have left these concepts untranslated. I hope the following discussion will make clear the principal Confucian uses of these concepts without constructions of English equivalents. Our discussion of *jên* in Section 4A owes much to the insightful study of Wing-tsit Chan, "The Evolution of the Confucian Concept *Jên,*" 295–319. All quotations from Chan cited in the text refer to this study.
6. References in the text of this chapter are taken from James Legge's translation of the *Analects,* in volume 1 of *The Chinese Classics.*
7. Chan notes that in the *Analects* "58 of the 499 chapters are devoted to the discussion of *jên* and the word appears 105 times." This frequency of occurrence is by itself an indication of the central importance of *jên* to Confucius. Its uses, as it were, control the unity of the discourses (p. 296).
8. Wheelwright, *The Burning Fountain.* For a recent discussion of the expressive character of Chinese language and thought, see Wu, "Chinese Language and Chinese Thought."
9. Compare this distinction with Thomas Aquinas' notion of "derivation": "Something may be derived from the natural law in two ways; first, as a conclusion from premises, secondly, by way of determination of certain generalities. The first way is likened to that by which in sciences, demonstrated conclusions are drawn from the principles; while the second mode is likened to that whereby, in the arts, general forms are particularized as to details: thus the craftsman needs to determine the general form of a house to some particular shape." "Treatise on Law," Question 95, Art. 2.
10. Chan, "The Evolution of Concept *Jên.*" Chan cites other evidence on p. 298. It is interesting to observe that all the remarks referred to appear to be instances of Jp and particular virtues.
11. This and the following quote from Hardie, *Aristotle's Ethical Theory,* 329.
12. See Hume, *Principles of Morals,* 7.
13. Hutcheson, *An Inquiry into the Origin of our Ideas of Beauty and Virtue,* 222.
14. Butler, *Fifteen Sermons,* 187.
15. Field, *Moral Theory,* 153.
16. In this section of the chapter we are concerned primarily with the relation of *jên* and *li.* Undoubtedly, the Confucian concept of *li* requires separate study, particularly in view of its central importance in the writings of Hsün-tzu.

Here we present only a brief outline of some aspects of this important Confucian doctrine. For a recent sympathetic evaluation of *li,* see Fingarette, *Confucius—The Secular as Sacred.* Also Cua, "The Conceptual Aspect of Hsün-tzu's Philosophy of Human Nature."

17. Waley's introduction to his translation *The Analects of Confucius,* 67.

18. Fingarette, "Human Community as Holy Rite: An Interpretation of Confucius' *Analects,*" in *On Responsibility,* 166.

19. Watson, *Hsün-tzu,* 21, 20, 87.

20. The terms "ethics of character," "ethics of rule," and "ethics of role" are adopted from Mayo, "The Moral Agent." For the significance of the concept of role for ethics, see also Emmet, *Rules, Roles and Relations* and Downie, *Roles and Value.*

21. Mayo, "The Moral Agent," 47–48, 49.

22. If my interpretation of *li* as embodying rituals for the performance of social roles is correct, we may here note its connection with the Confucian doctrine of *cheng ming* or rectification of names. To Confucius, the social roles have, so to speak, their own *proper names;* the ritual rules have their own proper linguistic formulas. To "rectify a name" in the Confucian sense is in part to make one's action conformable to the social roles through the invocation of appropriate ritual formula. The connection between *li* and *cheng ming* deserves further exploration, for it points to the intimate relation between Confucian ethics and politics.

23. Fingarette, *On Responsibility,* 174.

24. Ibid., 175.

25. Whitehead, *Modes of Thought,* 48.

26. As Waley pointed out (*Analects,* 35–38), the Confucian notion of *chün-tzu* resembles the Western ideal of a gentleman. McGee recently described this ideal: "The gentleman as defined by tradition aspired to nothing less than becoming a concrete universal. Guided and sustained by his limitation, he took as his moral ideal the cultivation of humanity.... His conduct was judged by its appropriateness, a measure that took account of particular circumstances, but always in conformity to the human ideal. Conduct regulated by this form felt congruous and fitting, hence purposeful. In the widest sense of 'manners,' the manner of the gentleman were the textures of his life, a texture isomorphic with the structure of his class." *Recovery of Meaning,* 222.

Chapter 5

1. Liu, *A Short History of Confucian Philosophy,* 11. See also Ware's introduction to his translation, *Analects,* 7; Creel, *Confucius and the Chinese Way,* 137; Hummel, "Some Basic Moral Principles in Chinese Culture," 601; Lin, *The Pleasures of a Non-Conformist,* 109; Fung, *A History of Chinese Philosophy,* 1:74.

2. Unless otherwise indicated all references in the text of this chapter are taken from the *Analects* translated by James Legge, *The Chinese Classics,* vol. 1. For a further discussion of sagehood in a later Confucian Hsün-tzu, see Cua, "Reflections on Methodology in Chinese Philosophy," 236–48.

3. This is Legge's translation. See also Chan, *A Source Book in Chinese Philosophy.* I have adopted this rendering of *"chün-tzu"* as "superior man."

4. See Waley, *Analects.*

5. For other remarks on *i* or righteousness, see *Analects,* I.13; VII.3; XII.20; XIII.4; XV.16; XVI.10 and 11.

6. Fung, *A Short History of Chinese Philosophy,* 42.

7. We here follow Chan's translations and commentary (p. 24). Also *Analects,* IX.6.

8. *Chung Yung,* ch. 12 and 14. See Legge, *Chinese Classics,* vol. 1.

9. The complete passage runs as follows: "The men who have retired to privacy from the world have been Po-î, Shû-chî, Yü-chung, Î-yî, Chu-chang, Hûi of Liu-hsiâ, and Shâo-lien. The Master said, Refusing to surrender their wills, or to submit to any taint in their person:—such, I think, were Po-î, and Shû-chî. It may be said of Hûi of Liû-hsiâ and Shâo-lien, that they surrendered their wills, and submitted to taint in their persons, but their words corresponded with reason, and their actions were such as men are anxious to see. This is all that is to be remarked in them. It may be said of Yü-chung and Î-yî, that, while they hid themselves in their seclusion, they gave a license to their words; but in their persons, they succeeded in preserving their purity, and, in their retirement, they acted according to the exigency of the times. I am different from all these. I have no course for which I am predetermined, and no course against which I am predetermined" (*Analects,* XVIII.8).

10. Austin, *How to Do Things with Words,* 81–82.

11. See *Analects,* XIII.3 and *Hsün-Tzu: Basic Writings,* 139–56. For a sketch of this doctrine of rectifying names, see Cua, "Reasonable Action and Confucian Argumentation," 57–75.

12. See Fingarette, *On Responsibility,* ch. 7.

13. Chan, *A Source Book in Chinese Philosophy,* 26; cf. Fung, *A History of Chinese Philosophy,* 1:74.

14. These renderings of *"ching"* and *"ch'uan"* are taken from *A New Complete Chinese-English Dictionary* (Hong Kong: Chung Chien Co., n.d.).

15. I have taken some liberty in presenting this doctrine of *ching ch'uan* with a view of making this doctrine more plausible and interesting for moral philosophy. I hope that reflective Confucian moral agents who, like myself, were reared in the tradition that places its major emphasis on the *Analects* will agree with this manner of presenting what I regard as one major insight of Confucius into the nature of moral experience.

16. *Mencius,* bk. I, pt. II, ch. 8. See Legge's *The Chinese Classics,* 1:167.

17. *Mencius,* bk. IV, pt. I, ch. 17.

18. Austin, "A Plea for Excuses," in *Philosophical Papers,* 179.

19. For this distinction, see Taylor, *Normative Discourse.*

20. James, *Essays on Faith and Morals,* 326.

21. This notion of functional equivalence of concepts or linguistic expressions appears to underlie Bruce Aune's explication of the notion of functional characteristics in his *Knowledge, Mind, and Nature.* Aune provides an instructive example: "Unlike the formal analogy between a red triangle and a certain sort of visual image, the analogy between uses of the English 'It is raining' and the German *'Es regnet'* does not concern their material (their phonemic or orthographic) features but the jobs they do or the roles they play in discourse. To the extent that these empirically different uses do play analogous roles in English and German, there is a sense in which the roles they play are abstractly the same. This 'abstract sameness' is what is involved when one says that the English 'I' and the French *'je,'* and the German *'Ich'* all play the role of a first person singular pronoun" (p. 184).

22. We may observe here that if there in fact exist functionally equivalent moral concepts or principles in two distinct moral practices, then it would seem

to follow that an acknowledgment of the rational or reasonable acceptability of one set of concepts would seem to argue for the same acceptability of the functionally equivalent one. For a critical study of Richard Price, see Cua, *Reason and Virtue.*

Chapter 6

1. Linton, "Universal Ethical Principles: An Anthropological View," in Ashen, *Moral Principles of Action,* 658. The terms "moral practice" and "morality" are used interchangeably here.

2. Hart, *Concept of Law,* 86.

3. Cf. Whiteley, "On Defining 'Moral,'" 141–44. The two points of view roughly parallel Whiteley's sociological and psychological points of view of morality. Our stress in this discussion centers on the interplay of these two points of view from the *position* of a reflective moral agent. This position, though typically an internal point of view in Hart's sense, recognizes also the legitimacy of the external point of view as also available to adoption of the moral agent within the moral practice. When a moral rule, which was previously accepted as authoritative, becomes subject to doubt or criticism, the agent may shift to an external point of view, regarding the rule as an item on an agenda for deliberation, i.e., as a statement subject to criticism. Its *de jure* status is so to speak suspended pending further consideration and bestowal of its authority. This is my point in saying that the difference between the two lies in a difference of emphasis. Of course, a moral agent cannot adopt both points of view *at the same time.* The adoption of one at one time precludes the adoption of the other. The difference, from the position of the agent, lies in the difference in the roles of actors and critics, not the difference between the roles of agents and spectators.

4. See Rawls, "Two Concepts of Rules," 1. Rawls regards a practice as "any form of activity which defines offices, roles, moves, penalties, defenses, and so on, and which gives the activity its structure. As examples one may think of games and rituals, trials and parliaments."

5. Waismann, "Verifiability," in Flew, *Logic and Language,* 120.

6. *The Works of George Berkeley,* 6:34. The distinction between open or complete and incomplete notions is derived from Kovesi's *Moral Notions.* Kovesi, however, thinks that there are complete moral notions like lying and murder. It is doubtful that there are many terms which function in this way. Confucian ethics, in particular, seems to be dealing with open rather than complete notions. I suggest that where situations normally fall within the scope of moral rules, the moral notions involved may be regarded as complete notions, in the sense that they provide a complete description and determination of the nature of the situations. In the absence of actual confrontations with problematic situations, moral notions are open notions. For pedagogical purpose we may treat them as complete notions since the understanding of these notions is constituted solely by examples and precepts, hypothetical or actual. However, where the situations call for a judgment of relevance of moral rules, the moral notions remain open to individual construction.

7. Finlay, *Axiological Ethics,* 13.

8. Singer, *Generalization in Ethics,* 9.

9. Kovesi, *Moral Notions,* 93. See also Nowell-Smith, *Ethics,* 267–70.

10. For a plea for the importance of the study in the logic of application, see Cua, "Toward an Ethics of Moral Agents," 163–74.

11. Henceforth we shall use the term *moral principles* in the sense of basic and superordinate rules. The italics signify this use. In this sense, a *moral principle* may not be accepted by an agent as *his* moral principle, as noted in Section 6A. We shall use the term "moral rules" leaving its basic or derivative status an open question.

12. Pole, *Conditions of Rational Inquiry,* 131, 146.

13. Hare, *Language of Morals,* 67.

14. Pole, *Conditions of Rational Inquiry,* 112. See also Whiteley, "On Defining 'Moral,' " 24–25; Warnock, *The Object of Morality,* 132ff.

15. Horsburgh continues, "The weaker criteria are determined from this strict criterion by a process of stretching or dilution of meaning. These criteria shade into one another forming a descending scale of strictness. There are only two additional formulations, however. These are: (1) *A* accepts a moral rule if (a) he intends to obey it, and (b) his intention to obey is unconditional. (2) *A* accepts a moral rule if (a) he wishes to obey it, and (b) his wish to obey it is unconditional." "The Criteria of Assent to a Moral Rule," 353–54.

16. This is analogous to perceptual consciousness discussed by Price in his distinction between perceptual acceptance and perceptual assurance. See Price, *Perception,* ch. 6 and 7.

17. Wittgenstein, *Philosophical Investigations,* para. 219.

18. Ibid., para. 85.

19. This strategy for dealing with uncertain situations is reflected in some contemporary philosophers' conceptions of moral rules and principles. See, for instance, Hare, *The Language of Morals,* 51–54, 63–65, 73–76; Singer, *Generalization in Ethics,* 103; Baier, *The Moral Point of View,* 192–93; Frankena, *Ethics.* For a more recent statement, see Gert, *The Moral Rules,* 68.

20. Singer, *Generalization in Ethics,* 24.

21. Cf. Baier, *The Moral Point of View,* 193.

22. Urmson, "Saints and Heroes," in Melden, *Essays in Moral Philosophy,* 212. For other criticism of the doctrine of built-in exceptions in the description of moral rules, see Melden, *Rights and Right Conduct,* 42–44; Murphy, *The Theory of Practical Reason,* 118, 194ff., 207–8; and Urmson, "Utilitarianism," 74–75.

23. Hare, *The Language of Morals,* 65.

24. Wittgenstein, *Zettel,* para. 294.

25. Mayo, *Ethics and the Moral Life,* 63.

26. Foot, "When is a Principle a Moral Principle?," 108–9.

27. Wittgenstein, *Philosophical Investigations,* pt. II, 226.

28. Ibid., pt. I, para. 241.

29. See Beardsmore, *Moral Reasoning,* ch. 10.

30. Aristotle, *Nocomachean Ethics,* bk. II, 1104a. This is also a common claim of deontological intuitionists from Richard Price to W.D. Ross. For a further discussion of this theme, see Cua, *Reason and Virtue,* ch. 4.

31. Anscombe, "Modern Moral Philosophy," in Wallace and Walker, *The Definition of Morality,* 229–30.

32. Perelman and Obrechts-Tyteca, *The New Rhetoric,* 197.

33. Ibid., 198. These remarks on reasonable moral agents merely draw attention to one dimension of reasonableness in terms of an agent's sense of acting in a manner fitting and appropriate to *his* situation. A reasonable agent probably would also pay heed to his moral practice, be watchful of self-regarding considerations in terms of his ideals and their possibility of realization within the bounds of his capacity and the reality of the situation, be open to evidence

for assessing his beliefs in light of evidence, and be sensitive to others' beliefs and feelings. For relevant discussion on the significance of the notion of reasonable men, see Aristotle, *Nicomachean Ethics,* bk. VI, ch. 5; Dennes, "An Appeal to Reason"; Nielsen, "Appealing to Reason"; Lucas, "The Philosophy of the Reasonable Man."

34. For an attempt in this direction with specific reference to Confucian ethics, see Cua, "Reasonable Action and Confucian Argumentation" and "Uses of Dialogue and Moral Understanding."

35. Urmson, "Utilitarianism," 74.

36. Miller, "Rules and Exceptions," 262.

37. Murphy, *The Theory of Practical Reason,* 230.

38. Urmson, "Utilitarianism," 75. See also Mish'alani, "Rules and Exceptions in Morals," 112.

39. Kant, *Critique of Practical Reason,* pt. I, bk. III, ch. 3. Trigg, "Moral Conflicts."

40. May, *Love and Will,* 13.

41. See Strawson, "Social Morality and Individual Ideal."

Chapter 7

1. On respect for persons: MacLagan, "Respect for Persons as a Moral Principle"; Williams, "The Idea of Equality," in Laslett and Runciman, *Philosophy, Politics and Society;* Harris, "Respect for Persons," in De George, *Ethics and Society;* Stock, *Morality and Purpose,* 40–48; Downie and Telfer, *Respect for Persons.* On legal theory: Fuller, *The Morality of Law,* 162; Stumpf, *Morality and the Law,* 237–38.

2. Kant, *Foundations of the Metaphysics of Morals,* 47. His influence is particularly evident in the full length treatment of the topic in Downie and Telfer's book. See also Williams', Stock's, and Harris' essays.

3. Stock, *Morality and Purpose,* 47. Also Williams, "The Idea of Equality," 117–18.

4. Kant, *Foundations of the Metaphysics of Morals,* 46. See also Kant's *Metaphysical Principles of Virtue,* 23.

5. This quote and the next: Kant, *Foundations of the Metaphysics of Morals,* 53.

6. Ibid., 18; *Critique of Practical Reason,* 83, 80; see also 79–81.

7. For an explication of the conception of generic as distinct from idiosyncratic characteristics along the Kantian line, see Downie and Telfer, *Respect for Persons,* 19–23.

8. Marcel, *The Philosophy of Existentialism,* 10.

9. Williams, "The Idea of Equality," 116–17.

10. This notion of the style of performance corresponds to Downie's notion of "qualities of role-enactment." See "Roles and Moral Agency," 41.

11. For the notion of intrusive novelty, see Pepper, *World Hypotheses,* 256.

12. All quotations in this paragraph from Horsburgh, "The Plurality of Moral Standards," 332–33. See also Mayo, *Ethics and Moral Life,* 216.

13. For psychological studies on levels of aspiration, see Kurt Lewin, *A Dynamic Theory of Personality* (New York: McGraw-Hill, 1935), ch. 8.

14. Hume, *Principles of Morals,* 7.

15. Wittgenstein's remark on the double usage of "particular" and "peculiar" appears to apply also to "original." "On the one hand . . . it is used as preliminary to a specification, description, comparison; on the other hand, as what one

may describe as an emphasis." *The Blue and Brown Books,* 158.

16. Glenn Langford, "Rules, Moral Rules and the Subjects of Moral Predicates," 196.

17. Schapiro, "Style," in Tax, *Anthropology Today,* 278.

18. These remarks on Alfred Adler are primarily based on his mature work *Social Interest.* Similar themes have been discussed in his *Understanding Human Nature, What Life Should Mean to You, Problems of Neurosis,* and *The Education of Children.* Useful passages from Adler's remarks on SL are gathered in ch. 7 of *The Individual Psychology of Alfred Adler.* Quotations in this paragraph are from *Social Interest: A Challenge to Mankind,* 11–12, 24, 93, 202, 286, 26–27, 75, 39.

19. Quotations in this paragraph are from Adler, *Understanding Human Nature,* 29; *What Life Should Mean to You,* 57, 57–58 (italics added).

20. Adler, *Social Interest,* 42–43, 276.

21. For a recent account and assessment of Adler's works, see the comprehensive work of Henri E. Ellenberger, *The Discovery of Unconscious,* ch. 8.

22. For an illuminating discussion on moral dilemmas as distinct from technical problems, see Phillips and Mounce, *Moral Practices,* ch. 8.

23. Paton, *In Defense of Reason,* 127. Paton explains: "The universal rule is that our actions should contribute and be willed as contributing to our happiness as defined above, but there is a whole system of subordinating rules into which this ultimate rule is articulated." Paton rightly notes that "the ordered unity of such a life is more than mere obedience to a rule, just as it is in the case of particular enterprise." We would much prefer to regard the universal rule as an ideal telos that implicitly governs a life plan, rather than as a supreme moral rule functioning in the way in which our moral practice does. The ideal telos in this case we regard as a norm for governing conduct, but not necessarily a supreme rule to which all moral rules are subordinated. An individual may have an ideal norm without a hierarchy of norms. He may be an idealist without a specific hierarchy of values. In my view, the question of value height is an open question for any moral agent, although a normative theory may attempt to prescribe the value height itself.

24. For both critical and sympathetic response, see, for instance, John Steinbeck's "The Trial of Arthur Miller" and R.H. Rovere's "Arthur Miller's Conscience," in Girvetz, *Contemporary Moral Issues,* 97–105.

25. Hare, *Freedom and Reason,* 88.

26. Merleau-Ponty, *Phenomenology of Perception,* 450.

27. James, "Moral Philosophy and the Moral Life," in *Essays on Faith and Morals,* 206.

28. Tolstoy, for instance, takes Christian love as "a law of love" (*Law of Love and Law of Violence*). Love can be taken in this way as a rule of benevolence, but what concerns us here is its interpretation as an ideal norm or theme. The Confucian *jên* or human-heartedness, as noted earlier, can be taken in either sense (see Section 4A).

29. Strawson, "Social Morality and Individual Ideal," 283.

30. Hare, *Freedom and Reason,* 77.

31. See MacLagan, "Respect for Persons as a Moral Principle," 209–17.

32. See Strawson, "Social Morality and Individual Ideal," 282.

33. Ayer, *Origins of Pragmatism,* 41.

34. Iris Murdoch, "Vision and Choice in Morality," in Ramsey, *Christian Ethics and Contemporary Philosophy,* 208.

35. See Cua, "Uses of Dialogue and Moral Understanding," sec. 2.

36. Goodman, *The Languages of Art,* 248.
37. Finlay, *Discipline of the Cave,* 29.

Chapter 8

1. James, "What Makes a Life Significant?" in *Essays on Faith and Morals,* 304, 305.
2. For convenience we follow the psychological terminology of cognitive, conative, and affective aspects in talking about ideals in general. For a careful analysis of these aspects of purposive behavior, see Pepper, *Sources of Value.* It should be noted that all three aspects are perhaps conjointly present only for a commitive moral agent, for one can have an intellectual vision of moral excellence without a full active commitment to its realization. Also, it is possible for one to commit oneself without feeling or emotion in executing the ideal task. This is in part the reason why we center our attention on the cognitive aspect of ideals.
3. Brightman, *Philosophy of Ideals,* 71. Brightman discusses the various cognitive features in much greater detail based on a descriptive definition of "ideal" as "a general concept of a type of experience which we approve" (ch. 3). I have merely drawn attention to cognitive features that bear on our distinction between ideal norms and ideal themes without following Brightman's normative definition of "ideal" as "a general concept of a type of experience which we approve in relation to a complete view of all our experience, including all our approvals" (p. 82). We reject the implication that all moral agents have such a comprehensive and inclusive telos. The normative definition applies more to certain agents' espousal of ideal norms rather than ideal themes. Even in the case of ideal norms, as previously pointed out, some agents may simply have a plurality of policies of life rather than a unitary telos (see Section 7D).
4. Olson, "On Avoiding the Void," 82.
5. For an illuminating discussion of this aspect, see Hare, *Freedom and Reason,* ch. 9.
6. Brightman, *Philosophy of Ideals,* 64.
7. Phillips and Mounce, *Moral Practices,* 101, 103.
8. For a detailed and illuminating discussion of the contributions of self-realization ethics, see Pepper, *Sources of Value,* ch. 17, *Ethics,* ch. 8, 9.
9. Wheelwright, *The Burning Fountain,* 81.
10. Jung, "Stages of Life" in *The Structure and Dynamics of the Psyche,* 395. Jung's emphasis on the midlife crisis contrasts with Adler's conception of life's problems. Whereas Adler regards the psychic difficulties of some people's lives as essentially problems that call for solutions in terms of an ideal norm of "social feeling," Jung stresses the importance of religion. Perhaps religions in general can also be regarded as providing ideal themes in addition to systems of norms and beliefs. So construed, religion can have a powerful contribution to make in providing answers to perplexity indicators.
11. May, *Love and Will,* 171.
12. For an early formulation of the distinction between knowledge by description and knowledge by acquaintance, see Russell, *Problems of Philosophy,* ch. 5.
13. Cf. Harrison, "Creativity and Understanding," 115.
14. Mill, *Utilitarianism,* 45–47. For an illuminating account of the various sources of value mutation, see Pepper, *Sources of Value,* ch. 7.
15. Hartmann, *Ethics,* 1:197.
16. Kant, *Critique of Pure Reason,* 486.

Bibliography

Adler, Alfred. *The Education of Children.* Chicago: Henry Regnery, 1970.
———. *The Individual Psychology of Alfred Adler.* Edited by Heinz L. Ausbacher and Rowena R. Ausbacher. New York: Harper Torchbooks, 1956.
———. *Problems of Neurosis.* New York: Harper Torchbooks, 1964. (Rpt. of 1929 edition.)
———. *Social Interest: A Challenge to Mankind.* New York: Capricorn Books, 1964. (1st English edition 1933.)
———. *Understanding Human Nature.* New York: Fawcett Publications, 1965. (Rpt. of 1927 edition.)
———. *What Life Should Mean to You.* New York: Capricorn Books, 1958. (Rpt. of 1931 edition.)
Aiken, Henry. *Reason and Conduct.* New York: Alfred A. Knopf, 1962.
Aquinas, Thomas. *Treatise on Law.* Chicago: Henry Regnery, 1962.
Aristotle. *Nichomachean Ethics.* Translated with an Introduction by Martin Ostwald. Indianapolis: Bobbs-Merrill, 1962.
Aschenbrenner, Karl. *The Concepts of Value: Foundations of Value Theory.* Dordrecht, Holland: D. Reidel, 1971.
Ashen, Ruth Nanda, ed. *Moral Principles of Action.* New York: Harper and Bros., 1952.
Aune, Bruce. *Knowledge, Mind, and Nature.* New York: Random House, 1967.
Austin, J.L. *How to Do Things with Words.* Oxford: Clarendon Press, 1962.
———. *Philosophical Papers.* Oxford: Clarendon Press, 1961.
Ayer, A.J. *Origins of Pragmatism.* San Francisco: Freeman, Cooper, and Co., 1968.
Baier, Kurt. *The Moral Point of View.* Ithaca, N.Y.: Cornell University Press, 1958.
Beardsmore, R.W. *Moral Reasoning.* New York: Schocken Books, 1969.
Beck, Lewis White. *A Commentary on Kant's Critique of Practical Reason.* Chicago: University of Chicago Press, 1960.
Bentham, Jeremy. *An Introduction to the Principles of Morals and Legislation.* New York: Hafner, 1948.
Bergson, Henri. *Two Sources of Morality and Religion.* New York: Henry Holt, 1935.
Brightman, E.S. *A Philosophy of Ideals.* New York: Henry Holt, 1928.
Butler, Joseph. *Fifteen Sermons.* London: G. Bell and Sons, 1953.
Castañeda, Hector-Neri, and Nakhnikian, George, eds. *Morality and the Language of Conduct.* Detroit, Mich.: Wayne State University Press, 1963.
Chan, Wing-tsit. "Chinese and Western Interpretations of *Jên* Humanity." *Journal of Chinese Philosophy* 2, no. 2 (1975).
———. "The Evolution of the Confucian Concept *Jên.*" *Philosophy East and West* 4, no. 4 (1955).
———. "The Evolution of the Neo-Confucian Concept *Li* as Principle." *Tsing Hua Journal of Chinese Studies,* new series 4 (1964).
———, tr. *Reflections of Things at Hand: The Neo-Confucian Anthology Compiled by Chu Hsi and Lü Tsu-ch'ien.* New York: Columbia University Press, 1967.

————, tr. *A Source Book in Chinese Philosophy*. Princeton: Princeton University Press, 1963.

Cheng, Chung-ying. "Yi as a Universal Principle of Specific Application in Confucian Morality." *Philosophy East and West* 22 (1972).

Confucius. *The Analects*. Translated by Arthur Waley. New York: Random House, 1938. (1st ed. London: Allen and Unwin, 1938.)

————. *The Sayings of Confucius*. Translated by James R. Ware. New York: New American Library, 1955.

Creel, H.G. *Confucius and the Chinese Way*. New York: Harper and Row, 1960.

Cua, A.S. "The Conceptual Aspect of Hsün Tzu's Philosophy of Human Nature." *Philosophy East and West* 27, no. 4 (1977).

————. "The Logic of Confucian Dialogues," in J.K. Ryan, ed. *Studies in Philosophy and the History of Philosophy*. Washington, D.C.: Catholic University of America Press, 1969, vol. 4.

————. *Reason and Virtue: A Study in the Ethics of Richard Price*. Athens: Ohio University Press, 1966.

————. "Reasonable Action and Confucian Argumentation." *Journal of Chinese Philosophy* 1, no. 1 (1973).

————. "Reflections on Methodology in Chinese Philosophy." *International Philosophical Quarterly* 11, no. 2 (1971).

————. "Toward an Ethics of Moral Agents." *Philosophy and Phenomenological Research* 28, no. 2 (1967).

————. "Uses of Dialogue and Moral Understanding." *Journal of Chinese Philosophy* 2, no. 1 (1974).

————, and Fletcher, J.J. "Paradigmatic Aesthetic Objects." *Man and World* 8, no. 2 (1975).

De George, Richard T., ed. *Ethics and Society: Original Essays on Contemporary Moral Problems*. New York: Anchor Books, 1966.

Dennes, William. "An Appeal to Reason." *Reason*, University of California Publications in Philosophy, vol. 27 (1939).

Downie, R.S. *Roles and Value: An Introduction to Social Ethics*. London: Methuen, 1971.

————. "Roles and Moral Agency." *Analysis* 29, no. 2 (1968).

————, and Telfer, Elizabeth. *Respect for Persons*. London: Allen and Unwin, 1969.

Ellenberger, Henri. *The Discovery of Unconscious: The History and Evolution of Dynamic Psychiatry*. New York: Basic Books, 1970.

Emmet, Dorothy M. *Rules, Roles, and Relations*. New York: St. Martin's Press, 1966.

Field, G.C. *Moral Theory*. 2d ed. London: Methuen, 1966. (1st ed. 1921.)

Fingarette, Herbert. *On Responsibility*. New York: Basic Books, 1967.

————. *Confucius—The Secular as Sacred*. New York: Harper & Row, 1972.

Finlay, J.N. *Axiological Ethics*. London: St. Martin's Press, 1970.

————. *Discipline of the Cave*. London: Allen and Unwin, 1966.

Flew, Anthony, ed. *Logic and Language, First Series*. Oxford: Basil Blackwell, 1952.

Foot, P. "When Is a Principle a Moral Principle?" *Proceedings of the Aristotelean Society*. Supp. Vol. 28 (1954).

Frankena, William K. *Ethics*. 2d ed. Englewood Cliffs, N.J.: Prentice-Hall, 1973.

Fuller, Lon. *The Morality of Law*. New Haven: Yale University Press, 1964.

Fung, Yu-lan. *A History of Chinese Philosophy*. 2 vols. Princeton: Princeton University Press, 1952.

————. *A Short History of Chinese Philosophy.* New York: Macmillan, 1950.

Gert, Berhard. *The Moral Rules.* New York: Harper and Row, 1970.

Girvetz, H.K., ed. *Contemporary Moral Issues.* 2d ed. Belmont, Calif.: Wadsworth Publishing Co., 1968.

Goodman, Nelson. *The Languages of Art.* Indianapolis: Bobbs-Merrill, 1968.

Hamilton, Edith, and Cairns, H., eds. *The Collected Dialogues of Plato.* New York: Pantheon, 1961.

Hampshire, Stuart. *Freedom of Mind.* Princeton: Princeton University Press, 1971.

————. "J. L. Austin, 1911–1960." *Proceedings of the Aristotelean Society,* 1959–60.

Hardie, W.F.R. *Aristotle's Ethical Theory.* Oxford: Clarendon Press, 1968.

Hare, R.M. *Freedom and Reason.* Oxford: Clarendon Press, 1963.

————. *The Language of Morals.* Oxford: Clarendon Press, 1952.

Harrison, Andrew. "Creativity and Understanding." *Proceedings of the Aristotelean Society,* Supp. Vol. 41 (1971).

Hart, H.L.A. *The Concept of Law.* Oxford: Clarendon Press, 1961.

Hartmann, Nicolai. *Ethics.* 3 vols. London: Allen and Unwin, 1932–50.

Holzman, Donald. "The Conversational Tradition in Chinese Philosophy." *Philosophy East and West* 6, no. 3 (1956).

Horsburgh, H.J.N. "The Criteria of Assent to a Moral Rule." *Mind* 62 (1954).

————. "The Plurality of Moral Standards." *Philosophy* 29, no. 111 (1954).

Hsün Tzu. *The Basic Writings of Hsün Tzu.* Translated by Burton Watson. New York: Columbia University Press, 1963.

Hume, David. *An Inquiry Concerning the Principles of Morals.* Indianapolis: Bobbs-Merrill, 1957.

Hummel, Arthur. "Some Basic Moral Principles in Chinese Culture," in Ruth Nanda Ashen, ed. *Moral Principles of Action.* New York: Harper and Bros., 1952.

Hutcheson, Francis. *An Inquiry into the Origin of our Ideas of Beauty and Virtue.* 3d ed. London: Printed for J. and J. Knapton, J. Darby, et al., 1729.

James, William. *Essays on Faith and Morals.* New York: Longmans, Green, 1949.

————. *The Varieties of Religious Experience.* New York: Longmans, Green, 1902.

Jaspers, Karl. *Socrates, Buddha, Confucius, and Jesus: The Four Paradigmatic Individuals.* Translated by Ralph Manheim. New York: Harvest Books, 1957.

Jung, Carl. *The Structure and Dynamics of the Psyche.* In *Collected Works.* Princeton: Princeton University Press, 1969, Vol. 8.

Kant, I. *Critique of Practical Reason.* Translated by L.W. Beck. Indianapolis: Bobbs-Merrill, 1956.

————. *Critique of Pure Reason.* Translated by N.K. Smith. London: Macmillan, 1953.

————. *Foundations of the Metaphysics of Morals.* Translated by L.W. Beck. Indianapolis: Bobbs-Merrill, 1959.

————. *Lectures on Ethics.* New York: Harper Torchbooks, 1963.

————. *Metaphysical Principles of Virtue.* Translated by J. Ellington. Indianapolis: Bobbs-Merrill, 1964.

Kierkegaard, Søren. *The Concept of Dread.* Princeton: Princeton University Press, 1967.

————. *Concluding Unscientific Postcript.* Princeton: Princeton University Press, 1968.

Klemke, E.D., ed. *Essays on Wittgenstein.* Urbana: University of Illinois Press, 1971.

168   *Bibliography*

Kovesi, Julius. *Moral Notions.* London: Routledge & Kegan Paul, 1969.
Kroeber, A.L. *Style and Civilization.* Berkeley: University of California Press, 1963.
Langford, Glenn. "Rules, Moral Rules, and the Subjects of Moral Predicates." *Proceedings of the Aristotelean Society,* new series 69 (1968–69).
Lao Tzu. *Tao Teh Ching.* Translated by T.C.H. Wu. New York: St. John's University Press, 1961.
Laslett, P., and Runciman, W.G., eds. *Philosophy, Politics, and Society, Second Series.* Oxford: Basil Blackwell, 1962.
Legge, James. *The Chinese Classics.* Vol. I–IV. Oxford: Clarendon Press, 1893.
Lin, Yu-tang. *The Pleasures of a Non-Conformist.* London: Heinemann, 1962.
Liu, Wu-chi. *A Short History of Confucian Philosophy.* New York: Dell, 1964.
Lucas, J.R. "The Philosophy of the Reasonable Man." *Philosophical Quarterly* 13 (1963).
Luce, A.A. and Jessop, T.E., eds. *The Works of George Berkeley.* 9 vols. London: Thomas Nelson & Son, 1949–57.
MacArmstrong, A. "Custom and Usage." *American Philosophical Quarterly* 2, no. 1 (1965).
MacDonald, Margaret, ed. *Philosophy and Analysis.* Oxford: Basil Blackwell, 1954.
MacLagan, W.G. "Respect for Persons as a Moral Principle." *Philosophy* 35, no. 134 and 135 (1960).
Marcel, G. *The Philosophy of Existentialism.* New York: Citadel Press, 1963.
Margenau, Henry. *Ethics and Science.* Princeton: Princeton University Press, 1964.
May, Rollo. *Love and Will.* New York: W. W. Norton, 1969.
Mayo, Bernard. *Ethics and the Moral Life.* London: Macmillan, 1958.
———. "The Moral Agent." Royal Institute of Philosophy Lectures, vol. 1, *The Human Agent.* New York: St. Martin's Press, 1968.
McGee, Douglas. *Recovery of Meaning.* New York: Random House, 1966.
Melden, A.I. *Rights and Right Conduct.* Oxford: Basil Blackwell, 1958.
———, ed. *Essays in Moral Philosophy.* Seattle: University of Washington Press, 1958.
Merleau-Ponty, M. *Phenomenology of Perception.* London: Routledge & Kegan Paul, 1962.
Mill, J.S. *Utilitarianism.* Indianapolis: Bobbs-Merrill, 1957.
Miller, Leonard. "Rules and Exceptions." *Ethics* 66 (1956).
Mish'alani, James K. "Rules and Exceptions in Morals." *Ratio* 11, no. 2 (1969).
Moore, G.E. *Principia Ethica.* Cambridge: Cambridge University Press, 1951.
Munro, Donald. *The Concept of Man in Early China.* Stanford: Stanford University Press, 1969.
Murphy, A.E. *The Theory of Practical Reason.* LaSalle, Illinois: Open Court Publishing Co., 1965.
Nielsen, Kai. "Appealing to Reason." *Inquiry* 1 (1962).
Nowell-Smith, P.H. *Ethics.* Baltimore: Penguin, 1954.
Olson, Warren E. "On Avoiding the Void: Ideals and Principles." *An Invitation to Phenomenology: Studies in the Philosophy of Experience.* Edited by J. Edie. Chicago: Quadrangle Press, 1965.
Paton, H.J. *In Defense of Reason.* London: Hutcheson University Library, 1951.
Pepper, S.C. *Ethics.* New York: Appleton-Century-Crofts, 1960.
———. *Sources of Value.* Berkeley: University of California Press, 1958.

————. *World Hypotheses.* Berkeley: University of California Press, 1942.

Perelman, C. and Olbrechts-Tyteca, L. *The New Rhetoric: A Treatise on Argumentation.* Notre Dame: University of Notre Dame Press, 1969.

Phillips, D.Z., and Mounce, H.O. *Moral Practices.* New York: Schocken Books, 1970.

Pole, David. *Conditions of Rational Inquiry: A Study in the Philosophy of Value.* London: Athlone Press, 1961.

Price, H.H. *Perception.* London: Methuen, 1932.

Ramsey, Ian T., ed. *Christian Ethics and Contemporary Philosophy.* New York: Macmillan, 1966.

Rawls, John. "Two Concepts of Rules." *Philosophical Review* 64, no. 1 (1955).

Rescher, Nicholas. *Conceptual Idealism.* Oxford: Basil Blackwell, 1973.

Resnik, M.D. "Logic and Methodology in the Writings of Mencius." *International Philosophical Quarterly* 8, no. 2 (1968).

Russell, Bertrand. *Problems of Philosophy.* London: Oxford University Press, 1912.

Ryan, John K. "Philosophy and Theology in a Discourse of St. Thomas Aquinas on the Incarnation and Christ the King," in *Studies in Philosophy and the History of Philosophy,* Vol. I. Washington, D.C.: Catholic University of America Press, 1961.

Saw, Ruth. *Aesthetics: An Introduction.* New York: Anchor Books, 1971.

Schopenhauer, Arthur. *Essays.* Translated by T. Bailey Saunders. Lincoln: University of Nebraska Press, 1964.

Shaftesbury. *An Inquiry Concerning Virtue or Merit* in *Characteristics.* Edited by S. Grean. Indianapolis: Bobbs-Merrill, 1964.

Singer, Marcus. *Generalization in Ethics.* New York: Alfred A. Knopf, 1961.

Stock, J.L. *Morality and Purpose.* London: Routledge and Kegan Paul, 1969.

Strawson, P.F. "Social Morality and Individual Ideal," in Ian T. Ramsey, ed. *Christian Ethics and Contemporary Moral Philosophy.* New York: Macmillan, 1966.

Stumpf, S.E. *Morality and the Law.* Nashville, Tenn.: Vanderbilt University Press, 1966.

Tax, Sol, ed. *Anthropology Today.* Chicago: University of Chicago Press, 1962.

Taylor, Paul. *Normative Discourse.* Englewood Cliffs, N.J.: Prentice-Hall, 1961.

————, ed. *Problems of Moral Philosophy.* Belmont, Calif.: Wadsworth, 1967.

Tolstoy, Leo. *Law of Love and Law of Violence.* New York: Holt, Rinehart, & Winston, 1971.

Trigg, Roger. "Moral Conflicts." *Mind* 80, no. 317 (1971).

Tucker, Robert C. "The Theory of Charismatic Leadership." *Daedalus* 99, no. 3 (1968).

Urmson, T.O. "Utilitarianism," in *The Isenberg Memorial Lectures Series.* East Lansing: Michigan State University Press, 1969.

Vessey, G.N., ed. *The Human Agent.* Royal Institute of Philosophy Lectures, Vol. I. New York: St. Martin's Press, 1968.

von Wright, Henrik. *Explanation and Understanding.* Ithaca, N.Y.: Cornell University Press, 1971.

Wallace, G., and Walker, A.D.M., eds. *The Definition of Morality.* London: Methuen, 1970.

Warnock, Geoffrey. *Contemporary Moral Philosophy.* New York: St. Martin's Press, 1967.

————. *The Object of Morality.* London: Methuen, 1971.

Weiss, Paul. *Modes of Being.* Carbondale: Southern Illinois University Press, 1958.

Wheelwright, Philip. *The Burning Fountain: A Study in the Language of Symbolism.* New and revised ed. Bloomington: Indiana University Press, 1968.

———. *Heraclitus.* New York: Atheneum, 1964.

Whitehead, A.N. *Modes of Thought.* New York: Putnam, 1958.

Whiteley, C.H. "On Defining 'Moral.' " *Analysis,* 1959–60. Reprinted in Wallace and Walker, *The Definition of Morality.*

Wittgenstein, L. *The Blue and Brown Books.* New York: Harper Torchbooks, 1958.

———. *Philosophical Investigations.* New York: Macmillan, 1965.

———. *Zettel.* Oxford: Basil Blackwell, 1967.

Wu, Joseph S. "Chinese Language and Chinese Thought." *Philosophy East and West* 19, no. 4 (1969).

Index

172 *Index*